Steel Closets

STEEL CLOSETS

Voices of Gay, Lesbian,
and Transgender Steelworkers

ANNE BALAY

THE UNIVERSITY OF NORTH CAROLINA PRESS *Chapel Hill*

*This book was published with the assistance of the
Anniversary Endowment Fund of the University of North Carolina Press.*

© 2014 THE UNIVERSITY OF NORTH CAROLINA PRESS

The University of North Carolina Press has been a member
of the Green Press Initiative since 2003.

Library of Congress Cataloging-in-Publication Data
Balay, Anne.
Steel closets : voices of gay, lesbian, and transgender steelworkers / Anne Balay.
pages cm
Includes bibliographical references and index.
ISBN 978-1-4696-1400-7 (cloth : alk. paper) — ISBN 978-1-4696-1401-4 (ebook)
1. Homosexuality—Indiana. 2. Gays—Indiana. 3. Lesbians—Indiana. 4. Transgender
people—Indiana. 5. Iron and steel workers—Indiana. I. Title.
HQ76.3.U52163 2014
306.76'609772—dc23
2013036921

18 17 16 15 14 5 4 3 2 1

THIS BOOK WAS DIGITALLY PRINTED.

IN MEMORY OF MY MOTHER,
Harriette Anderson Balay, 1929–2012.
Your hard work and your stories live on.

CONTENTS

ILLUSTRATIONS

ACKNOWLEDGMENTS

I owe this book, and everything else, to my daughters: Emma and Leah. I thought that I would teach them about the things that matter: books, school, love, rainy days. And that happened. Then they turned around and taught me about courage. Thanks for raising me.

I was also helped by countless friends, colleagues, and strangers. I could not have survived the five years I spent researching, writing, and revising *Steel Closets* without the support of John D'Emilio, Jimbo Lane, Ginger Costello, Bob Balay, Steve McShane, Arryn Hawthorne-Jader, Robin Rich, Carina Pasquesi, Jerry Davich, Tracy Baim, and Jesse Weaver Shipley. And the energy, support, and insight my students have contributed make it all worthwhile. Indiana University Northwest denied me promotion and tenure as I finished the book, which made the steelworkers' hostile work environment uncomfortably personal, but they funded me for two summers off first, for which I am grateful. At the University of North Carolina Press, editorial director Mark Simpson-Vos and my readers—Steve Estes, E. Patrick Johnson, and an anonymous reviewer—transformed the book with their patient, insightful feedback. I thank them all voluminously.

Riva Lehrer, my partner, renews my belief in the honor of hard work and my respect for people and bodies in all their gorgeous variety. Thanks for sharing stories and sunrises with me.

Finally, this book is for the steelworkers. I have some sense of the guts it took for them to sign the consent form and open up their hearts and histories to me so I could share them with others. For that, and for their lives packed with hardship and beauty, I am eternally grateful.

Steel Closets

Introduction

In a 1997 episode of *The Simpsons* called "Homer's Phobia," Homer Simpson becomes convinced that his son, Bart, might be gay. In response, he takes him to a steel mill. He intends to show Bart what a "real" man is and does, but the joke is on Homer when the steelworkers break into a disco chorus line number on lunch break. They're all gay.

This is one example not only of how powerful the metaphor linking steel production and masculinity is in our culture, but also of how gay men function as a pivot point in that definition. Much of the traditional folklore of the American nation involves steel and its production. John Henry was a steel-driving man, Superman is the Man of Steel, and steel is a crucial component of the Empire State Building, the transcontinental railroad, the Golden Gate Bridge, highways, automobiles, and other American icons. Steel is both a material and a metaphor for the construction of the nation; it is part of the idealized American spirit. In all of this larger-than-life mythology, masculinity and heterosexuality are assumed, yet, as "Homer's Phobia" ironically reminds us, queerness can never be completely dismissed.

If steel is central to the mythology of America as a whole, it's even more dominant in Northwest Indiana. Plenty of American towns have been shaped by the steel industry—Pittsburgh, Bethlehem, Birmingham, Youngstown, Buffalo, and Baltimore among them. Gary, Indiana, and its environs resemble these towns in many ways and take their rust-belt attributes to further extremes, offering a rich example of the connection between the myths of steelworkers and general heteronormative notions of labor.

Steel Closets asks where and how steelworkers—those archetypes of working-class masculinity—and gay folks overlap. Stereotypically, queer people (I use this term as shorthand to represent those whose sexual preference or gender presentation does not fit the norm) flee to urban centers to escape prejudice and find others like ourselves. Further, American culture tends to assume that queers are middle-class, white, and educated. Scholars are beginning to challenge these assumptions—people such as Jack Halberstam, Scott Herring, E. Patrick Johnson, and John Howard, for example, study queers who have chosen not to relocate to northern cities, and instead stake out ways to be gay where and how they live. This book contributes to this growing body of research, focusing specifically on how steelworkers experience and embody their gay identity at work. Since queerness is a minority identity that people can (usually) hide, the choice of whether, how, and when to become visible, and what it means to name and lay claim to that identity need to be given a rich context in order to be understood. *Steel Closets* aims to provide a deep background about working, social, and family life and then present the stories and lives of queer steelworkers as they unfold within it.

To accomplish this goal, in 2010 and 2011 I interviewed forty gay, lesbian, and transgender steelworkers, mostly in and around Gary, Indiana. Northwest Indiana is the only place in the United States where basic steel is still made in huge, traditional production mills. These mills are "a man's world"—both the job itself and the culture surrounding it preserve their traditional shape. I learned that gay people are profoundly invisible in that world—and isolated and scared. Yet the forty people I interviewed told stories not only of danger and hard labor, and resistance to change, but also of community and pride and an important job well done. These forty people, my narrators, chose to use aliases to conceal their identities, but they embraced the chance to share their lives and stories—to be heard, seen, and valued. Throughout this book, italics are used when I'm quoting from one of these interviews. A comment from Danielle exemplifies the flavor of these complicated stories: *"Things are a little bad, rumors and stuff get there before you arrive. But I do my job, I do it as best I can, usually there's no problem. The only problem I have right now is lotta people are homophobic. They really don't do anything to me personally, but you'll see things like 'faggot' written on a board, the usual slang, ways to try to tick you off, but I just don't let it bother me."* All of the narrators face this kind of prejudice—and often significant personal danger—but don't let it define them—and they know that their experiences matter and that people in the wider public should have a chance to learn about their challenging, adventurous lives.

I have never worked in a mill, and consequently, as I drive by the mills on the highway, they seem alien and ominous. They smell, emit smoke constantly, and display a forest of high chimneys capped by methane burn-off flames. Some of the photographs in this book are intended to give a sense of the scale, the beauty, and the danger of the steel mills. Some were taken by me or by friends, and some are from the Calumet Regional Archives at Indiana University Northwest. The people depicted are not my narrators, and

This is as close as you can get to U.S. Steel. Gary Works is visible
in the background, 2012. Photograph by Patrick Bytnar.

I'm certainly not suggesting that any of the people in these photographs are queer by including them. Rather, the photos are presented because they enable viewers to visualize humans in these alien spaces as they change through time. The mills have actually changed extensively—so much so that the air in Gary stinks a lot less than it did as recently as twenty years ago—but they still look the same: the physical/built environment of the mills remains consistent and foreboding. They look like something out of a bad science fiction movie, or like dinosaurs. They look like stasis—the outright refusal of progress.

Working in one of the mills is like falling out of time. Mills preserve an old-school macho culture that, while changing, also reinforces itself constantly. It's a given that change causes backlash, and that cultural shifts engender resistance from conservative forces. In the mills, such social resistance to change is echoed and reinforced by physical isolation and by material, daily reminders of the past.

The culture of the mills is rife with resistance to progress of many kinds, including environmental regulation, ethnic diversity, women's employment, and advances in industrial practice. This atavistic character is demonstrated by the mills' hostility toward all change, including twenty-first-century America's increasing cultural acceptance of gay people. Within basic steel mills (which is what the vast, start-to-finish steel mills that dot the Northwest Indiana coast of Lake Michigan are called), GLBT people continue to be harassed, abused, *and* expected to remain invisible. The steelworkers I spoke to blame this hostility to gay people on two factors: the physical isolation of the mills and the hazardous and communal nature of the work. Extremes of heat and cold, volatile chemicals kept under pressure and located near fire, machines and vehicles in constant motion, and the sheer scale of the steelmaking process make mill work risky. And since the work is dangerous, co-workers depend on each other literally for their lives. A safety equipment sales representative remarked to me that each steelworker's goal is to go home at the end of the day. It's that simple—and that stark. Just as in combat situations or in prisons, this risk, combined with the spatial and emotional distance between the mills and the surrounding community, increases the bond between workers and makes differences among them undesirable.

Geographic isolation contributes to social isolation as well. Working in basic steel separates you from the rest of the community—you virtually disappear when you go to work. Even people who live and work near the mills generally don't know steelworkers intimately and often manage to forget that they exist. Marie reports that *"I didn't have what I would consider a lot of close friends. . . . When you work those kinds of shifts and those hours, it cuts you off from things that people might do normally."* The schedule, the risk, and the tradition keep mill life alien from everyday, modern life as most people know it. Xena describes this disjunction, observing: *"This is terrible to say, but the South Shore tracks run through where I work at, and you hit those tracks and the problems at home stay there and you begin your day at work."* Xena expresses regret about this isolation—she longs for a life less divided, where she doesn't have to be so careful about hiding at work. Norman agrees, citing the stress of *"keeping track of who knows what, and where you are. The mill, there's this whole set of rules. It might seem like a free-for-all, but us gays got to be careful out there. It's not safe."*

Steelworkers such as Andy describe feeling like soldiers returning from Vietnam—the community pretends not to see them so as to avoid responsibility. And this separation is caused by, and causes, the exclusion of gays: almost all of the workers I interviewed described measures they take to keep their mill selves and their "real," gay selves separate. In daily life, being gay infuses a person's identity and affects everything he or she does, but because the mills are so geographically, socially, and temporally isolated, workers have to shut down that aspect of their identity in order to make their already challenging jobs bearable.

Steelworkers in the twenty-first century routinely walk through spaces little changed from the early twentieth century, and they blame this stability on the danger and isolation of mill work. Lakisha says her mill is *"like caught in time in a few places because there's a tunnel that you had to walk through to get from one side to another, and it's where the donkeys used to pull the carts, and no joke they still had the rail that the carts went on, and when you'd see that every day you just thought, wow, we haven't gotten very far."* Christopher Hall notes in *Steel Phoenix* that steel as an industry changes very slowly—things are done now in much the same way they were forty, and even a hundred years ago. Richard Dorson agrees, adding in his urban folklore account *Land of the Millrats*, that the process of making steel is "evolutionary rather than revolutionary" (46). Hugo provides confirmation of this slow movement, noting that mill work *was a tough life. Guys that worked in the coke ovens, where they're basically walking on top of ovens with wooden shoes on because everything else would burst into flames. . . . I don't think the coke oven technology has changed that much. I mean, they may be burning a little more efficiently, but they're basically stacks of these furnaces, and they put stuff in, one they literally open up the side, and the others they push into a railcar and it goes into a pit."*

This stasis gives steel mill work a fixed and rigid quality—since the structure and the process resist change, people tend to as well. In a rapidly changing world, this consistency makes mill workers even more isolated, and less integrated into mainstream culture. Of course, individual steelworkers weave modern technology into their lives—I have gotten countless Facebook posts and tweets from bored mill workers whiling away time on the job—and almost all mill jobs involve some interaction with a computer. Yet the isolation and protection of the work from outside influences comes into conflict with, and causes distance from, modern life.

When I envision a steelworker in this context, doing work that is dirty, dangerous, and disrespected, against the brutal scale of the mill and its machinery, it's easy to understand the vulnerability of any worker's body. A truck's tires are often as tall as the person who drives it. This image doesn't fit our idea of a modern American worker. Because the mill work setting is so physical, bodies—perhaps especially gay bodies—are radically exposed, which illustrates my narrators' situation in highly visual and visceral terms. Danielle describes this problem: *"And I was staying in the closet about who I really was. I was a very visible person, let me put it that way, I had to go to different parts of the plant to collect samples."* Her visibility—the long walks she takes alone to various, remote corners of the mill—display her body, which is one of the ways we communicate sexuality and other forms of identity. In this passage, she links her decision to remain closeted to her body as a spectacle—something looked at and therefore vulnerable.

Though social acceptance is increasing for many queers, working-class and poor gay people don't benefit from this change as much as urban, middle-class queers do. A 2012 interview quotes Amber Hollibaugh, now working as a community organizer in New York City, who asks, "Is it different to come out now than it was to come out thirty-five years ago? Sometimes. But if you come out now and you come from poverty and you come from racism, you come from the terror of communities that are immigrant, or where you're already a moving target because of who you are, this is not a place where it's any easier to be LGBT even if there's a community center in every single borough" (Flanders).

Being openly gay first gained widespread acceptance in the arts—painters, poets, actors, and musicians were queer pioneers, and there persists a nearly unbridgeable cultural gulf between artists and blue-collar workers. In addition, blue-collar life in America is closely linked to family iconography (think of the television show *The Middle*, for example, though popular culture images of blue-collar workers are scarce these days). Queer distance from traditional family structures can reinforce blue-collar discomfort with gay folks. For these and other reasons, the steelworkers I spoke to report that hostility to gay people still lingers in the mills long after it has begun to fade elsewhere, coercing their silence. This enforced silence, and the accompanying isolation, contribute to the impact of queer steelworkers' stories. Crafting and sharing a story is one way to gain control over the contradictions of being working-class and queer, and possibly a member of another minority as well, and many of my narrators weave powerful stories born of necessity and alienation.

The Book's Methodology and Origins

The steelworkers' stories that form the bulk of this book are stories born of fear, survival, and struggle. My training and professional experience are in English, so I approach these stories, words, and narratives using the tools of literary scholarship. The interviews I did are not only documents recording people's lives, but also words crafted into stories by means of which these same people made sense of their experiences, and communicated them to a wider audience. Thus, I'm a listener, but also a reader. In reading over the interviews, I sought out patterns, recurring themes, and significant words, phrases, or images. I combed through the transcripts like a literary scholar searching for meaning.

When I conducted the interviews, I let the steelworkers lead. I didn't want to sensationalize their experiences or shut down some stories by fishing for others. Typically, I just turned the tape recorder on and let them talk. Occasionally, they would prod me to ask a question to get them started. Nate's response to my initial prompt was typical. I asked him to describe what, specifically, he did on the job, to flesh that out for my readers. He responded with, *"I've always known I was a gay man"* and then proceeded to roll out a narrative of his life. To the same prompt, Fred replied, *"As little as possible."* Then he paused theatrically, laughing, thanked me for feeding him the "straight line" and began to relate his sexual and employment history.

I include these two representative preambles to emphasize that the steelworkers I interviewed are consummate storytellers who use narrative to construct and understand their lives. Because there was little relationship between my question and their responses, they must have had these stories prepared—probably had told them before. Like "coming out," they are narratives that provide the tellers with agency, voice, and opportunity to understand themselves in the context of their worlds. It is as stories that I relate and read them here, stories that, in both hearing and reading, performed powerful work on me. Often I got people to talk by sharing experiences I had had as a mechanic, and I encouraged them to continue by flirting, and by caring. I liked most of these people immediately, and I let them see that. And their stories moved me, shook me up, and redefined heroism for me.

Stories are power. As a literary scholar, I'm predisposed to capitulate to them. And these stories and tellers did a great job. As I read and reread the transcripts, I hear their voices still, and the truth of their experience shines through their words. As I read, themes and patterns emerged, constellated into chapters, and led to conclusions. Each interview is its own story—its own truth—complete with literary value, beauty, and pleasure. Seen together, the interviews form a chain of stories with historical significance that make possible a revised understanding of queer identity.

FIRST AND FOREMOST, this book tells the steelworkers' stories simply because the stories matter and they have not been heard. My research was sparked at an Indiana University Northwest faculty social hour in the fall of 2009 when Jim Lane, a newly retired regional historian, asked me whether I had ever considered having my students interview gay and lesbian steelworkers. He was excited by work he was doing in oral history and seemed happy to meet a real, live gay person to whom he could direct this question. Lane explained that he had assigned the task of interviewing gay steelworkers to a previous class as part of a social history project on the increasing visibility and voice of minority groups at work, but since those students weren't gay, they had had a hard time finding subjects, and an even harder time getting them to disclose their experiences. He imagined queer steelworkers had a particularity of experience that was still untapped.

I was immediately intrigued. I'm a lesbian, and I had previously worked as a car mechanic, so I had some experience as a woman in a traditionally male occupation—one that offers more dirt and danger than respect—which increased my interest in what interviews with steelworkers might reveal. Though Gary's main street, Broadway, looks like a war zone, and though many people who live in Northwest Indiana don't realize that steel is still made here, five huge mills and various smaller ones continue to operate, and they employ many people. It stands to reason that some of these workers are gay, lesbian, bisexual, or transgender. Initially, I assumed I could begin exploring their experiences through traditional scholarly research.

I turned to the library catalog and then searched academic journals, popular periodicals, and various databases for information about queer steelworkers, but found nothing. Indiana University Northwest houses the Calumet Regional Archives, one of whose specialties is the steel industry in the region. When I asked its curator, Steve McShane, whether he knew of any work on the topic, he didn't even pause to think about it—he had nothing about gay steelworkers of any kind. He suggested I try Rivers of Steel, an extensive, federally funded steelworking archive in Homestead, Pennsylvania, outside of Pittsburgh. I contacted a curator by email and set up an appointment to visit the site.

In Homestead, I met with the curator, Tiffany Ewing, and with the archive's manager, Ron Baroff. Both were more fascinated than they were helpful. They had reviewed their collection before our meeting and could find no mention of gay or lesbian steelworkers. Each reassured me that Pittsburgh was a very gay-friendly location, reminding me that the TV hit "Queer As Folk" was set there. To be identified as gay causes no problems in the Pittsburgh area, they both asserted. Yet I suspect that this accepting attitude does not apply to the Pittsburgh area's LGBT steelworkers: their utter silence speaks louder than words.

I concluded that the only way I could learn about the experiences of queer steelworkers was to ask them. Since I work in an academic setting, my university is responsible for guaranteeing that any people I use in my research are not abused, so I worked with the Human Subjects Committee to design a two-page consent form that each potential subject would have to read, understand, and sign.

I began seeking out steelworkers by going to the region's gay bars and asking around. I met my first narrator almost immediately, in November of 2009. He signed the form and then told me stories. And what stories they were! I have a good memory, and I took copious notes immediately, but that interview convinced me that I needed a voice recorder, and permission to tape conversations. While this added another step to my consent process, it also made much longer interviews feasible.

Since I was obligated to conceal narrators' identities and to disguise names, ages, workplaces, and specific tasks as needed, I decided to give each narrator an alias, working alphabetically from A to Z. These aliases are the names I use in the book. Readers can learn a bit more about each narrator in the appendix. When I quote from the interviews, I try to capture each steelworker's language and word choice exactly. Verbal style is more casual than written language, but correcting grammar or eliminating profanity would take the flavor out of the stories. As I read through their narratives, I hear their voices, and each regional and ethnic dialect is worth preserving.

Initially I had hoped to use what sociologists call snowball sampling, in which one narrator can lead to many more; I imagined that each time I met a GLBT steelworker, I could ask that person to contact his or her friends and suggest that they talk to me. However, I soon learned that gay steelworkers are too hidden for such a technique to succeed. Most folks I interviewed believed they were the only gay person working in basic steel. Trying to avoid detection themselves, they occasionally suspected that another worker was "like them," but they never asked outright. Many were shocked that I had found others and were incredulous that so many not only existed but were willing to come forward. A few reported recognizing a co-worker at a gay bar, and two of my narrators told someone else to contact me, but overwhelmingly, each GLBT steelworker worked alone. The mill work environment effectively keeps gay people isolated, unable to connect.

So I used every avenue I could think of to meet steelworkers. I kept going to bars. I visited local gay-friendly churches. I discussed my work in every possible context, knowing that contacts come from unexpected places. I reached out to Labor Studies faculty. I contacted gay and regional media, hoping for exposure. And everything worked. Total strangers in bars, secretaries in other departments at my university, journalists, and friends of friends all helped me. Still, I felt like I was squeezing blood from a stone. After fifteen months, I had only sixteen consented, transcribed interviews. But they were amazing. These people had stories that would make your blood run cold. I learned that working in a steel mill is a lot like being in combat. The danger and isolation of the job create a bond between co-workers. You survive out there only if you have toughness, strength of character, and a sense of humor. But then, it has always been true that being gay in our culture increases the chance of experiencing teasing, loneliness, harassment, molestation, and rape. These people had survived all that, and more. And they did not whine or complain—they handled their work and their lives with pride, with laughter, and with inspiring nobility. I *had* to tell their stories.

So I recontacted Jerry Davich, a popular local feature columnist who had mentioned my work in passing before. I suggested we meet for lunch, discuss my progress, and see if he found enough material to write a full profile. He did. His column appeared in the *Northwest Indiana Post-Tribune* on January 24, 2011. My name and phone number were included in the column. This led to hostile voice mails, and even a few death threats. My favorite was from a woman saying she had worked in the steel mills for thirty years and could guarantee that only Christian people, and no disgusting perverts like me, worked with her. Hindsight lets me see the irony in this claim because that same day, seven "disgusting perverts like me" called and left contact information so that I could subsequently interview them. And that was just the start.

When my interviews began, I thought I knew what it was like to work in a hostile environment and to face fear every day at work. In fact, I knew nothing. Even the most hostile, gay-bashing student evaluations, the most malicious overheard comments, and inexplicable denial of tenure are nothing compared to direct threats to your life and safety, or to those of your children. This experience increased my respect for the gay steelworkers who endure similar experiences every day, without complaining and without insulting *or even disliking* the people who create and foster this hostile environment. Their blend of survival, generosity, and humor gives me hope and inspiration.

Ultimately, forty people became my narrators. They ranged in age from nineteen to their early sixties. Most still worked in a mill, though four had moved on to other jobs, two were currently laid off, and one was retired.

There were twenty men and twenty women, with a decent amount of racial diversity, at least among the women. Nineteen of the men are white and one African American, while fourteen of the women are white, two African American, three Latina, and one Asian. I use various terms to describe my narrators' sexualities or orientations. The narrators themselves tend to use the term "gay," with the women typically calling themselves "gay women." I follow this pattern, and also use "queer" when I want a term that encompasses various manifestations of outcast gender and sexual expression.

AS I CRISSCROSSED NORTHWEST INDIANA doing these interviews, hearing these stories, meeting these people, I was constantly reminded of the human capacity to endure trauma. There were times when I had to take breaks—to stop the interview process for a while because I just couldn't absorb any more. Yesenia described coming home from work to find her partner (also a steelworker), overwhelmed and depressed by a lifetime of struggle, holding a gun, which she then turned on herself and fired. Though Yesenia (a trained medic) tried to resuscitate her, her partner died. *"I did the whole therapy thing, did the whole psychiatrist thing. I'm still on medication. She messed me up, y'know?"* Her speech is choppy when she tells this story, and she's fighting back tears. The daily personal cost of bigotry, both to her partner and to herself, is palpable in this story.

When she went back to work, could this steelworker tell her co-workers why she couldn't stop shaking and looked like hell? How many stories of rape, violence, harassment, and outright hostility can one person hear? And yet hearing them is obviously less horrible than living them, while still mustering the strength to get up, go to work, and find a way to be who you want to be. Can we give these people a world where this requires less struggle?

I BELIEVE THAT MY NARRATORS were willing to share their stories with me partly because I'm queer and partly because I had been a mechanic—I not only understood but also had lived their struggle. I noticed that I had much better luck meeting steelworkers in bars when I wore my mechanic's uniform jacket. Professors, maybe especially English professors, tend to make working people uncomfortable. Mechanics, on the other hand, work with tools, dirt, and grease. Steelworkers recognize auto mechanics as people who share some of their conditions of work, and their outlook. One narrator showed me a vintage car he had stopped restoring because of a work-related injury. Right away, I noticed that he got stalled trying to separate a tie rod, and I could bond with him about pickle forks, cotter pins, axle grease, etc. More commonly, my experiences with rolling around on a creeper, trying to get grease off my hands, having hot oil run into my armpits, solvents, work-arounds, long johns, and injuries created common ground, and even a sense of easy friendliness.

These shared experiences also helped me to respect the steelworkers— to want to know more about the nitty-gritty of the steelmaking process and how people learn to do that work and how they feel about it. I knew enough not to understand, but to ask appropriate questions, and that built trust. For example, though there were challenges to being a female mechanic, I believe being a lesbian made these easier, for reasons similar to those the female steelworkers I interviewed describe. Though I'm not a hardcore butch, few people would describe me as feminine. At my interview, the service manager surveyed my body type and remarked with approval that the standard uniform wouldn't need to be tailored to fit me.

When I was hired, the other staff consisted of two young black men: Jonathan James, called Poo, and Maurice Lee, called Mo. Poo told me very early on that his perception of his own work, and his sense of status in the community, dropped precipitously when I was hired. Poo told me this knowing it was insulting, but he felt the need to say it anyway. In researching this book, I came to understand that his reaction was very similar to that of male steelworkers when women entered the mills. One account in "Calumet Regional Steelworkers' Tales" (a collection of oral histories of steelworkers published by James Lane in 1990) observes, "It's hard to go home and tell your wife or mother or girlfriend, 'Boy, I'm really working a rough job' when the woman can do it" (82).

It helped ease the tension between us that Mo and Poo had been there a while, they knew the procedures, and they were training me. Having greater knowledge and seniority gave them the status advantage they needed to be able to handle working with a woman. But my being a lesbian was not a problem, and they accepted it easily. I'm guessing they assumed it based on the fact that I applied for and took the job, a decision they thought no straight woman would make.

We had a regular parts deliverer whom we didn't like. He was always in a rush and had an inflated sense of his own importance. On April Fool's Day, Poo got a "barely legal" (a porn magazine in the worst possible taste) and covertly slid it into this guy's delivery vehicle. While I was not supposed to know this, I had had ample opportunity to overhear. The next day, when the delivery van arrived, I went up to the driver as he came through the shop. Acting sheepish and embarrassed, I confided that the guys had given him my magazine, and said that I'd like it back. More than anything, his reaction of stupefied disgust gained me the respect of my co-workers. Like many lesbian steelworkers, I was thus able to gain respect and fit in with my co-workers because of our shared interest in women, and my willingness to play that up.

There is a custom among mechanics that you can ask parts distributors or dealers for "girlfriend rates" or "girlfriend parts." The understanding is that you want to impress "your" woman by demonstrating insider access to, say, high-performance struts, but that you don't want to spend much money to do so. I could easily call in and request girlfriend parts from these people without challenging their worldview. If I had tried to institute a new policy of "boyfriend parts" they would have had to think about my femaleness—to acknowledge that a woman was at home in their world. Being a lesbian made me at once unremarkable and interesting.

This background—my hands, my self-presentation, my jacket, my sense of humor—all made me part of a blue-collar world, and therefore easy to talk to. My working-class background placed me outside the stereotype of the white, urban, professional queer—a stereotype that, as Scott Herring argues in *Another Country*, is often used prescriptively to define what counts as gay (5). Consequently, it made me approachable to other people excluded from that narrow, hegemonic "lifestyle."

I used personal contacts to connect with queers in Northwest Indiana, a region geographically close to the urban center of Chicago, but still remote in terms of behavior, style, and sociality (Herring 21). For example, in the spring of 2010, a former student called me to tell me she was competing in a drag event at the area nightclub that evening. I arrived and located Tami, who was already dressed and looking nervous. The entertainment began with performances by several regular drag queens at this bar. Then the emcee for the evening announced the commencement of the male impersonation competition and introduced the judges. We watched as four drag kings took the stage. Multilevel platforms had been arranged for the contestants to stand on, and they posed while the emcee read off their names and brief "bios." Though they did a lot of posing and strutting, each contestant was obviously nervous at this point.

After several more drag queen numbers, each king came out individually for the formal wear competition. The emcee carefully described the designer, color, and source of each tuxedo, and the contestants were instructed to rotate in front of the judges. The contestants were silent, using gestures and facial expressions to convey masculinity. My former student, contestant #3, wore an "ensemble derived from Valparaiso Good Will"; another mutual friend quipped to me about contestant #4's tuxedo: "so totally rented."

The contestants still seemed amateurish and awkward. Contestant #2 had an especially hard time holding character—her nervous smile kept breaking through.

The platforms were then removed; "burly lesbians from the audience" were solicited and volunteers (including me) did the work. More drag queens performed, including Miss Gay Bar 2009, almost the only black person in the bar. Then, before the talent competition began, the emcee reminded the audience that contestants could not be tipped during their numbers or they would be disqualified.

This portion of the competition is where the contestants relaxed, eased into their roles, and had fun. In the first number, the contestant lounged before a TV, flipping channels and drinking beer. When he flipped to a song about masculinity, he got up, adjusted his clothes in accordance with the lyrics, and then eased into the musical performance. Contestant #4 stole the show. Before the curtain opened, a child's plastic John Deere ride 'em toy had been placed on stage. The song was Kenny Chesney's "She Thinks My Tractor's Sexy," and the contestant wore cowboy boots, a flannel shirt, jeans with a bandana suspended from his belt loop, and a straw hat. Contestant #4, whom I will call Guy, was able to both have and mock masculinity effectively. The size of his "tractor," his evident comfort with and enjoyment of masculine style, and his dance moves combined with flirtatious eye contact, drove the audience wild. Toward the end of the number, two drag queens came onstage and proceeded to compete for Guy's attention, and for access to the tractor.

When winners were announced, after a few more drag queen performances, contestant #3, my student, won the interview portion and Mr. Congeniality, but first prize went to Guy. He was crowned Mr. Gay Bar 2010, complete with a tiara and sash. The bar owner came out to congratulate him and the emcee listed the people he would like to thank; Guy posed for countless photos with officials from the evening's performance and then "sang" a final number, during which tipping was allowed. Guy, contestant #4, basked in the attention, obviously thrilled with winning. A substantial cash prize accompanies the victory, in addition to the glory of the title, Mr. Gay Bar 2010.

Contestant #4 is a steelworker.

Though she never agreed to be interviewed, we have kept in touch. Her story doesn't appear in the following pages; it stands in for the silence that this book is a first step toward ending. Fear, habitual invisibility, cultural devaluation, and simple busyness prevented many potential narrators from talking to me. Yet this silence itself is one way of being queer, and including it and the voices of the forty who did sign the consent form constitutes a crucial addition to scholarly and public understandings of what it means to be queer. It's easy to leave people like Guy out of the story of gay life because they are silent. Rather than commanding media attention, working-class gay folks often try to remain invisible. Further, they don't conform to current understandings of what it means to be gay. Each person I interviewed identified as gay but didn't fit the mold of out, proud, queer identity. Yet that's not a reason to exclude them, as much as it's a reason to change the mold.

Finally, working-class queers, at least as manifest in the steelworkers I interviewed, are not part of the narrative of queer liberation—for them, it doesn't get better. The increasing visibility of, and legal protection for, gay people in our culture creates a backlash in the mills, making variations from traditional gender roles or sexual identifications less welcome, and more threatening.

These reasons notwithstanding, working-class queers are a crucial part of the story of twenty-first-century gay identity. They challenge our assumptions about what it means to be gay in important and interesting ways. Work, social, and sexual identities are not separate, and these and other working-class GLBT people's stories need to be a part of how we see and understand queerness.

Steel Closets tells such stories, drawn from my conversations with the forty steelworkers who signed the consent form. These forty are only a fraction of the gay steelworkers I met, and they, in turn, are only a fraction of the total population. Seen as a group, these stories and silences suggest numerous conclusions, each of which I will explore more fully in the coming chapters.

Conclusions and Implications

Chapter 1 provides background on the region of Northwest Indiana, its mills, and its culture. Building from there, Chapter 2 argues that as technology reduced the size of the workforce, it brought more idle time and more personal contact, which made it harder for gay folks to remain invisible.

These chapters demonstrate that, as LGBT people gained more national visibility and political clout, it became harder to be quietly, unremarkably gay at work. Since this cultural shift happened at the same time that numerous plant closings and widespread downsizing occurred, increasing tensions intensified harassment and exclusions of queers.

Chapter 3 explores how and why most queer steelworkers remain closeted at work. Many steelworkers describe lives of fear, while others tell of experiencing harassment, violence, or rape. All steel mill work is dangerous, but the risks increase, and cause more acute stress, for workers who are seen as different.

Chapters 4 and 5 relate the experiences of female and then male gay steelworkers. I analyze the genders separately because, in the mill, male and female queers are not in parallel situations. Since the mill work culture traditionally forms around talking about women and bragging about sex, lesbians fit in much more easily than do our gay brothers, though gay men's experiences are also shaped by this macho culture. Many of the men I interviewed have sex with other men at work, but their partners don't identify as gay. The mill is an environment in which men can give and receive oral sex without seeing themselves as queer. This culture makes it harder for gay men to come out at work, since their partners would then have cause to question their own behavior and identification.

Danger and illness are topics I take up in Chapter 6. Even aside from accidents and injuries, mill work frequently causes long-term health problems such as cancer and alcoholism, many of which exist already at higher than normal rates in queer populations.

Chapter 7 concerns the union. Most steelworkers I interviewed believe that the union to which most of them belong—the United Steelworkers (USW), formerly the United Steelworkers of America (USWA)—concentrates on keeping mill jobs safe and pay satisfactory. It does *not* protect gay steelworkers from harassment and violence.

In the epilogue, I relate stories about steelworkers in Canada, where things aren't as different as we might expect. I also discuss why, given the extensive challenges and dangers queer steelworkers experience, they persist in the work. Though other good-paying jobs are few, these steelworkers also have a commitment to mill jobs, and mill lifestyle, that goes beyond mere salary considerations.

As these and other conclusions emerge from the steelworkers' stories, one nearly constant theme is how work—the jobs people do, how, and why—effects how we see ourselves, including how we understand sexual orientation and gender identity. My narrators tell many stories that describe what workers need to do to make sense of themselves in a workplace: they watch the other workers to see what behaviors and attitudes fit—what "works." Thus, the work context and work culture generate a certain behavior and identity. It is within that context that what it means to be masculine, and what it means to be working-class, emerges. As John Howard claims in his study of mid-twentieth-century gay men in rural Mississippi, "Notions and experiences of male-male desire are in perpetual dialectical relationship with the spaces in which they occur, mutually shaping one another" (xiv). Howard would agree that this is true of all desire—all pleasure—which can't be understood apart from the spatial context in which it emerges. In addition, mill work shapes the bodies of its workers. Steelworkers have strong hands and bad hearing. There is dirt under their fingernails and ground into the grain of their hands. The mill shapes behavior, too: steelworkers tend to be aware of what is around them and very alert, queer ones maybe even more so. Work shapes all workers, and work in a basic steel mill influences you to become the type of person who works in a basic steel mill.

Judith Halberstam's work on Brandon Teena, the transman whose life and death are told in the film *Boys Don't Cry*, led her to realize "how little we actually know about the forms taken by queer life outside of metropolitan areas" (*In a Queer Time and Place* 35). Halberstam states that "Most queer work on community, social identity, and gender roles has been based on and in urban populations, and exhibits an active disinterest in the productive potential of nonmetropolitan sexualities, genders, and identities" (34). Halberstam calls for an expanded archive of "things not seen"—for research that we didn't even know we didn't have yet. This book is one step in that direction, not only adding a piece to what we think of as gay identity, but also suggesting a revision of what it means to identify as gay anywhere.

CHAPTER ONE

Setting the Scene

During the twenty-first century, tolerance for and even acceptance of gay and lesbian people has increased. President Barack Obama's public support for gay marriage preceding his reelection in 2012 and the Supreme Court's DOMA ruling in 2013 are prominent markers of this shift. Yet this change is not consistent or universal. Anti-trans violence is still common, and queer teens are bullied to death regularly. And most of the GLBT steelworkers I interviewed do not feel safe enough to come out at work, fearing rejection, violence, and dismissal, among other consequences. Their stories back up these fears. This chapter explores what it is about steel mills—the work, the location, the people, the history—that makes them so inhospitable to queers, even as the culture in which they are set becomes more accepting. Our sense of what it means to be queer remains incomplete until we understand and include these people and their experiences.

The mills are huge, physically remote structures, covering many acres. They are frightening, mysterious, beautiful anachronisms. A powerful, almost prehistoric magic adheres to them, like a fine gray dust. And it adheres to steelworkers as well.

A Century of Steel

The first mills to come to Northwest Indiana were Inland Steel in East Chicago (1901) and United States Steel (USX) in Gary (1906). Both plants were built on largely unsettled land, situated near Lake Michigan and thus convenient to barge and rail transport of raw materials from the Mesabi Iron Range in Minnesota and from Canada, and both towns were built for the workers who arrived to construct and then work in the mills. Youngstown Sheet and Tube was founded in 1923, right across from Inland. The Bethlehem Plant in Burns Harbor (1964) and National Steel in Portage (1960) were the last basic steel mills built in the area. All these mills are now owned by ArcelorMittal (an international conglomerate) except Gary Works, which is still owned by U.S. Steel.

Excavation for open hearth, U.S. Steel, Gary, 1906.
Courtesy of the Calumet Regional Archives.

What a basic steel mill does is both simple and hugely complicated, largely due to issues of scale. Steel has two main ingredients: iron ore and carbon, which often comes in the form of a by-product of coal called coke. The goal is to heat the iron ore enough to get impurities out of it and to make possible its chemical bond with carbon. This then becomes iron. Next, the resulting molten metal must be combined with other agents (lime, for example) and poured into billets or else continuously cast into finished product. Early on (since the late 1800s) this heating was done through the Bessemer process. The large, curling black smokestacks visible in most steel mills persist from this time, though they are no longer in use. Open-hearth furnaces, blast furnaces, and the Bessemer process were how steel was made in the basic steel mills in and around Gary until late in the twentieth century. Gradually, after that, each plant switched over to the currently used basic oxygen furnaces (BOFs). While the Bessemer process blows air through iron to purify it, which takes about twelve hours per (large) batch, BOFs blow just oxygen through the iron, which takes a fraction of the time (as little as forty minutes). Additionally, BOFs require much less labor, so as they became standard, each mill's worker pool could become correspondingly smaller without reducing output.

The steelworkers I interviewed believe that the mills in Northwest Indiana waited too long to make this modernizing switch, thus lessening their competitiveness with foreign-made steel. Indeed, open-hearth furnaces were still being built in the region long after they were no longer state-of-the-art. Further, continuous casting was slow to catch on in area mills, though it is now standard. In continuous casting, steel is produced, refined, and poured as part of one, uninterrupted process, rather than being cast into billets and then remelted to be rolled or pressed later.

What remains constant in the basic steel process is this: iron ore is delivered, heated to very high temperatures, then combined with carbon and other chemicals as needed; slag (impurities resulting from this process) is poured off, and the steel is poured, rolled, cut, coated, and otherwise prepared for market; it is then labeled and stored until it gets shipped, either by rail or truck. The slag must be disposed of somehow, often in slag heaps on mill property.

Steelworkers perform many of these jobs remotely now. Mechanization and increased efficiency mean that many steelworkers sit in pulpits, which are small glass-walled rooms overlooking the mill floor. There, they observe huge machines, watch readouts on monitors, and wait for something to go wrong. At any given moment, there are only a few workers on the mill floor, performing maintenance tasks, or getting a closer look at some piece of equipment. Other workers service the many machines and computers on the floor. Some work in labs, performing chemical tests on the product, and others monitor safety. Many move things around—coils of steel, loads of coke or slag, pieces of equipment, hot slabs that need to be cut. Emergency workers are always on site, as are cafeteria workers and janitorial staff. All the work is dirty, loud, and dangerous, because of particles in the air and because of the constant risk of explosion from impurities (such as water) in the product. And though the process has been modernized and now can be done by fewer workers, it remains in many ways consistent across time and between mills.

Over the course of the twentieth century, demand for steel continued to increase, though the type of steel required gradually shifted from heavier to lighter product, as consumer goods such as cars, appliances, and even food cans gained precedence over train tracks, locomotives, and I-beams. While many plants, such as those in Pittsburgh and Baltimore, have shut down, the four large mills in Northwest Indiana continue to produce huge volumes of steel. Yet, because the workforce is greatly reduced and at least the noticeable pollution lessened, the work that goes on there is increasingly less visible, even within the region. Nevertheless, what steelworkers made and how they made it has remained crucial to the myth-making that has defined "America," despite the fact as the twentieth century progressed, steel production (and all industry and manufacturing work) lost economic dominance and cultural capital. Jobs in technology, entertainment, and the service sector began to define the ideal America, while mills were seen as smelly, dirty polluters, preferably not visible from stylish urban centers, and perhaps even better located overseas.

No one factor makes integrated steel mills different from other industrial or factory workplaces, and consequently more hostile to queers. Several circumstances, in combination, distinguish steelworkers and the tasks that they do from workers in an auto plant, a garment factory, a nuclear power facility, or an oil refinery. The isolation of the mills (both physically and socially), immediate and long-term danger to workers, the cooperative structure of work within a mill, and the glacial pace of change within the industry all contribute to this difference. Danger and cooperation will be discussed in subsequent chapters, while the more geographic factors will be explored here. Taken together, these differences prove significant for the people who work there, especially the gay ones.

First, the mills are deliberately kept apart from the towns that they border. Several sets of train tracks snake between the mills and the urban centers of Northwest Indiana. Signs warn people not to cross these tracks unless they are on authorized business. Then, there are guarded gates. Some workers have permission to enter and park inside the mill, but most instead drive to parking lots several miles away, where they catch buses into the mill. These buses are gray so that the dust they collect in the mill proper will be less visible. A workplace so controlled that even its workers are bused in takes its isolation very seriously.

Second, most workers take showers at the end of their shifts. Some jobs require showering as a means to reduce the spread of toxic chemicals out into the community. Other jobs simply provide showers, which most workers use to reduce the filth spread to their cars and homes. Even with showers at work, many homes in the region come equipped with a shower in the basement. In a *Wall Street Journal* article, the journalist Robert Matthews described how many workers enter their homes through the basement door and shower again before heading upstairs to join their families. This tradition of showering at work, typically in an open room with no privacy, is another factor that makes working in a basic steel mill unique.

U.S. Steel transport buses, 2012. Photograph by Patrick Bytnar.

Finally, most mills, though modernized, are fundamentally the same structures that were built a century or more ago. Workers describe working in essentially the same place, doing the same job as their grandfathers. They describe rats, raccoons, and beavers who now treat the mill as a part of the natural environment. The daily routines of these workers and the equipment that they use have remained hauntingly constant.

Historians of steel mills and workers within those mills agree that this longstanding stasis is reinforced by the fact that basic steel mills have modernized little since the 1980s; this is one reason the U.S. steel industry has struggled in recent decades. In countries like Austria, Finland, and Brazil, steel profits were spent (at least in part) on technical improvements that increased productivity and safety. In the United States, as workers like Marie point out, our mills stayed the same, apparently believing they could continue to succeed *"by doing the same things in the same way they had always done."* Resistance to change, then, characterizes the physical space of the mills and rubs off on the people whose lives are shaped by them.

Many workers I interviewed talk about the weight of the past and its impact on their lives. Hugo, for example, describes the system by which clothes are stored in the locker room. *"There'd be hooks all around these rooms, that'd go up and you could unlock it, and let the rope down, and this chain comes down, and you'd hang your clothes and boots on this chain, and then you'd haul it back up, so it looked like there were 100 people hung from the ceiling because your boots would be the last thing you'd hook on the chain. . . . So when you'd arrive to change into your work clothes, the boots are all hanging there. . . . It was the strangest sight . . . Kinda ghostly."* This routine sight of hanging bodies is more than a convenient storage system. It's also a reminder—a static, palpable, visceral reminder—of the risk of fatality that is an ongoing reality of mill work. In this description, and in so many of the steelworkers' anecdotes, risk and resistance to change are linked. Tradition, repetition, and ritual help stave off anxiety, while simultaneously serving as reminders of danger, and as re-enforcers of social stasis.

Shift work creates another level of isolation. Most steelworkers work alternating turns: one week of 7:00 A.M. to 3:00 P.M., one week of 3:00 P.M. to 11:00 P.M., and one week of 11:00 P.M. to 7:00 A.M. The rotation continues ad infinitum. This makes social interaction with non–mill workers difficult. You can't be part of a regular bowling team, for example, because of how irregularly you have to be at work. It is very difficult to schedule day care in such a way that your kids are supervised during your shifts but you're still able to spend time with them when you're not working. Therefore, parents (especially mothers) are unlikely to take more time away from home for social interactions. And people who aren't part of the culture don't really understand how the schedule works, or how it affects those who are locked into its cycle. Thus, steelworkers tend to interact chiefly with other steelworkers, to minimize irritation and stress.

Demonstrating that steel mills are isolated, slow to change, and stable begins to explain why the big integrated mills are so inhospitable to queers. When a community is permeable, and new people flow in and out of it regularly, or interact with its principal players in significant ways, it stands to reason that it would be more likely to change than a community that is closed, and therefore reinforces its inherited patterns. R. W. Connell attributes homophobia in working-class work settings to traditional family ideology and accompanying gender roles, which he notes persist in ethnic enclaves and isolated areas longer than they would in more mobile, heterogeneous communities (109).

In addition, steelworkers often do their work in pairs or groups, depending on their co-workers for their success and their survival, a situation that creates a certain solidarity, reinforced by the exclusion of difference (of some or all of women, blacks, ethnics, or queers). William Serrin has published a history of the Homestead Steel mills (outside of Pittsburgh) in which he observes that the communal nature of the work creates familiarity and uniformity (19). Olshana remembers: *"I had the feeling that when I was there, with such big things going on all around you I really think that people had a sense that their lives were in the hands of their co-workers, and you never knew when you would have to depend on that co-worker to do something that would save your life or get you out of the way. So you may not get along outside, or you may not hang out outside, but in the mill you were kind of forced to be attentive and co-operate with your co-workers, no matter who they were."* If your coworker might have to snatch you out of harm's way, you need to trust that person, which is a feeling that often derives from shared values.

Working partnerships and a sense of community are, then, crucial for safety, and they can be a significant source of pleasure as well. A woman quoted in James Lane's "Calumet Regional Steelworkers' Tales" points out that "in the mill you would be assigned to an experienced millwright and would basically just hang around with him for six or eight months. The two people would do everything together. They'd eat lunch and take their breaks together. The training partnership was a social relationship when it worked well. Just being a woman made that difficult" (69). Scholars Mary Margaret Fonow and Ruth Needleman have established, respectively, the challenges women and blacks confront in connecting to their white male co-workers, but the challenges are even stronger for queers, especially gay men.

Sense of community, camaraderie, and an easy-going, pleasant workplace depend, at least in part, on the absence of queers—at least visible ones. Michael Warner argues that our culture creates hierarchies of sex, and of shame, whose aim is to shut down sexual variance. He claims that all sex is demonized, but some acts of, or places for, sex are more privileged, and are granted a certain neutrality, or naturalness. In this context, those who stand out "become a lightning rod not only for the hatred of difference, of the abnormal, but also for the more general loathing for sex" (23). This process of shaming, in which deviance and perversion cling only to queer subjects, who can then be symbolically or literally excluded in order to make the dominant group feel united and normal, was repeated often in the stories steelworkers told me.

For example, Zach describes navigating the mill's group mentality and what happens if you don't fit in: *"We help each other at work so, to me it's still good. It is what it is. You know it could be a whole lot worse. . . . I mean, it could be horrible. . . . I'd say in that kind of environment, if they don't like you they're gonna make your life hell."* And Bernard, whose co-workers suspect he is gay, though he has never explicitly said so, has felt ostracized more often than not. In one incident, a manager *"was also belittling and harassing me that I'm not being manly enough to do the job. He would do it with an audience of people. I'd go to tell the section manager about it, nothing would change this man's behavior. The thing that came to a head, was October 21st, a 3:00 to 11:00 shift, I had went to the restroom, I was coming back to the tempered metal line, when Sal stopped me, he says, 'Nobody likes you, all the guys don't like you. You don't work with nobody, you don't help out, you're not participating, and everybody's going to go to management to have you kicked out in the sequence and put in labor or somewhere else in the mill.'"* Incidents like this one illustrate how groups of workers can create a sense of shared values through identifying a common enemy, and a person whose gender or sexuality doesn't fit the norm is often chosen for that position.

This targeting of sexual outsiders is possible, in part, because people in the twentieth century have identified "sexual orientation" as a meaningful component of identity—maybe *the* meaningful component. Eve Sedgwick observes that same-sex desire and behavior has "a long, rich history," and that what changed at the turn into the twentieth century was that "every given person, just as he or she was necessarily assignable to a male or female gender, was now considered necessarily assignable as well to a homo- or a hetero-sexuality, a binarized identity that was full of implications, however confusing, for even the ostensibly least sexual aspects of life" (2). Everyone—straight, gay, and otherwise—feels the effects of this change, as our "sexual orientation" defines who and what we are both broadly and deeply. Without this shift, it might have been possible to argue that being gay is irrelevant to job choice or work culture. As it is, being gay or lesbian isn't seen as something a person stops doing at work, since it sets the terms of possibility for myriad actions and conversations that bear no direct relation to sex or gender. Furthermore, being gay is not just one half of a binary, it's the stigmatized half—the "other" half—easy to blame or victimize since, as a minority, queers define what counts as "straight" simply by representing its opposite.

THIS BOOK EXPLORES the dynamic of sexuality and work by listening to GLBT steelworkers as they tell their stories. I should say that I did not start out with a specific sense of what constitutes a GLBT steelworker, or any GLBT person for that matter. People who came to me identifying themselves as GLBT, I took at their word. Many of those I interviewed had been in straight relationships, from which they had children. Two were in straight relationships at the time of our interview. I did not prod these or any of my narrators to discuss why or how they identified as gay—I simply took it as a given, since they had chosen to talk to me. Each person, merely by entering this conversation, became part of a queer counterpublic, accepting the stigma and acknowledging that he or she was not above the "indignity of sex" (Warner 35).

The interviews were very unstructured. Typically, once the steelworkers got started, there was no stopping them. Stories often poured out for hours. Sometimes I would raise certain topics if they hadn't touched on them already: gay community, union support, coming out, drugs. If they didn't take the bait, I didn't push. And, really, I didn't have to. All of the narrators had plenty to say when I simply let them wander.

Ben is a big guy, with a jocular, confiding manner. I interviewed him in my office, where it immediately became clear that he loves to tell stories and capture his audience's attention. He was dressed causally in jeans and a sweatshirt, and he adjusted his gut occasionally, for comfort. Chris was almost his opposite—thin, well-groomed, and precise. I interviewed Chris in his immaculate home, in which classical radio wafted from hidden speakers. Doug lived in a subdivision, in a home packed with antiques and paintings. He sported a large rhinestone earring and was eager to show me his artwork and discuss his antiquing adventures. Though none of these men were visibly gay, and I wouldn't have picked them out in a crowd since they were indistinguishable from "regular," working-class guys, each fit several gay stereotypes.

The women were more identifiably gay, though that may be because, as a lesbian myself, I have both more practice with and more stake in picking lesbians out in a crowd. Further, they had less need to hide and more pressure to appear masculine, both of which contribute to an identifiable butch look. Xena, for example, walked and talked like a lesbian. For the interview, we met in her house, which was decorated with a southwestern motif and smelled of cigarettes. When we subsequently met for drinks, the sight of her walking from her car to the bar left little doubt that she is a gay woman—there was a cockiness and stiff swagger to her walk that is unmistakable code to those in the know. Felicia had the same bandy, wiry legs, and cowboy swagger. Both wore feathered mullets. Fern, in contrast, had spiked hair with bleached tips. She wore a Ralph Lauren decorated leather jacket, which she never removed, and boots. For all the women, boots were standard, as were jackets, often advertising their mill or a sports team (the Steelers), or boasting fringe.

Most of the women came to my office, whereas men were much more likely to meet me in their home or in a public place. Perhaps the men were reluctant to enter potentially unsafe space, where they might be identified and then questioned. Perhaps women felt less confident welcoming a stranger into their homes or planning an encounter with one in public. Whatever the reason, I always let the narrator pick the location, which meant I was often driving out to some trailer park to meet a stranger to, among other things, discuss sex. I couldn't tell anyone where I was going, or when, because that would violate confidentiality. I don't have a cell phone. Though I had received implied and explicit death threats about my interviews, I simply chose to trust fate, and in fact nothing dangerous ever happened. The scariest interview was with Quentin, who kept his hand over his mouth the whole time. Though we were in a crowded, loud restaurant, he was himself so horrified by the story he was telling me that he couldn't seem to let it out. His self-silencing was hard to watch. Elise, whom I interviewed in her apartment, was also pretty frightening. She is a male-to-female steelworker, who I had worked hard to track down by phone. Though she had initially called me, when I called back, she didn't reply right away, and when she finally did, she was actively paranoid, alleging that someone had sent me to her from the news media. Her apartment was empty, except for a sofa and rows of brown paper bags full of documents. She showed me glossy photos of her surgery and of her postsurgery body, and then gave me lists of license plate numbers she wanted me to forward to the police, hoping I would help advocate for her regarding suspicious activity and stalking. The last hour of our interview brought riffs on paranoid themes, such as *"The ACLU won't call. And the FBI knows it. The people involved, that I got a complaint with, are basically all Jewish. I have to call the FBI. Are we going to be meeting again? I was just really adamant about it all. I saw the ad in the paper, if you can ask if my voice mails are deleted, someone deleted them. She's a spy, and she hates us types of people."* Even Elise, though clearly mentally ill, meant me no harm and provided me with detailed stories and analysis.

All the people I interviewed, whether male or female at the time of the interview, shared one feature: all seemed hard pressed to fit into the available space. If we were in my office, they shifted around a lot. In their houses, they smoked, got drinks, took me on tours, seemed always ready to bust out of confinement and find somewhere that provided more room for them to be themselves. Even in a bar or restaurant, they fidgeted. Whether this was anxiety, unfamiliarity, or simply excess energy, it gave an urgency and physicality to their stories—we were not just talking, but rather actively engaging in time and space.

My oral history technique—whom I talked to, where and how—combines strategies drawn from various scholars, including E. Patrick Johnson, whose book *Sweet Tea* presents long, detailed narratives by southern black gay men; Elizabeth Kennedy and Madeline E. Davis, whose *Boots of Leather, Slippers of Gold* gives a deep context for lesbian identity by linking together stories about lesbian social and bar life in Buffalo; and Studs Terkel, who presents edited accounts of American working life in *Working*, first published in 1974. Terkel opens *Working* with the story of Mike Lefevre, a steelworker employed at a basic steel mill in south Chicago, where he "handle[s] between forty and fifty thousand pounds of steel a day" (xxxi). Mike longs for "something to point to"—for a plaque on the Empire State Building, for example, listing all the workers who contributed to its construction. Instead, he feels bitterness and alienation due to "the non-recognition by other people" (xxxii). He is worried that computers will eliminate his job (he works at/as a "bonderizer"), and he believes that the public devalues his brain and potential, reducing him to the automaton that is his steel mill role. He wants a college education for his son, who he hopes will become "an effete snob," albeit one who has "a little respect, to realize that his dad is one of the somebodies" (xxv) who do manual labor. Even in 1974, a high point in basic steel in terms of wages, job security, and benefits, Mike feels angry and used.

It is no coincidence that Terkel opens by profiling a steelworker. Mike's wife works occasionally as a waitress, but she is usually at home. He has two children, one of each gender. He's a stereotypical, iconic American worker. One of the final accounts in *Working* is that of another steelworker, Steve Dubi, who asks, "What have I done in my forty years of work? I led a useless life. Here I am almost sixty years old and I don't have anything to show for it" (557). Though he sounds disappointed, Steve observes, "That job was just right for me. I had a minimum amount of education and a job using a micrometer and just a steel tape and your eyes—that's a job that was just made for me. But they don't appreciate it. They don't care" (557). Further, the job has both short- and long-term dangers: since "you have to eat all that dust and smoke, you can't work hard and live a long life" (557). Steve has a stay-at-home wife and two boys.

The workers I interviewed have much in common with these two men. They feel bitter, exhausted, devalued, and at risk. And their jobs fit these patterns as well. The mills employ fewer and fewer people, and more procedures are automated, but the work is still dirty, loud, dangerous, and dull. Since they are gay, lesbian, or transgender, the folks I interviewed also differ from Steve and Mike and have experiences that remain invisible in Terkel's and many other accounts written about steelworkers. But I will start by describing what they share with Terkel's steelworkers, so that readers can fit their jobs, lives, and stories within a setting and inside a history that make them intelligible.

Mill Work: The More Things Change, the More They Stay the Same

Steel mills had long smelled bad, emitted smoke and fire at all hours, and loomed large and mysterious on the margins of cities like Chicago or Philadelphia. The people who worked there had always been seen as lawless and out of control, if only because they were almost all men who made comparatively high salaries and kept unpredictable hours. Strip clubs, gambling facilities, and bars have always been ubiquitous near mills, and municipal authorities in surrounding communities have always worried about crime. Often, violence in the vicinity of the mills has included clashes across lines of race or immigrant status, as new waves of willing workers brought in to perform undesirable jobs began to jockey for housing and better work opportunities.

Most people who live in the shadow of the mills—who literally drive by them every day—know little of what goes on inside. And the general public knows even less. Who works in the mills? What do they do? The *Simpsons* episode discussed in the Introduction, Studs Terkel's framing of his oral histories with steelworkers' stories, and the role of Gary as an icon of American urban decay reflect how steelworkers and steel mills are an unknown, mysterious alien presence in American life. Learning about the mindsets of steelworkers, the choices they make, and the logic of their lives provides a window into a piece of American mythology.

As for any group, for steelworkers the logic behind their lives leads to realities that are often confusing and contradictory. The ways of being in the world determined by class, gender, and sexuality often overlap or come into conflict. My goal is, then, not to make sense of my narrators' stories, but rather to let their contradictions, their choices, their negotiations give voice to the complexities of their lives. Violence and danger permeate working-class life in visceral and immediate ways that the rest of the population does not typically experience. What effect does that tendency have on how and where people play out their sexual stories? There is a heightened lore around risk-taking among my steelworkers, partly because of the sense that life is short and partly due to compulsory masculinity. To oversimplify, when people feel powerless (for reasons of class, race, age, etc.) risk-taking is one means of giving voice to that loss of control, as illustrated by almost anything ever recorded by Bruce Springsteen. Furthermore, many pleasures, both sexual and otherwise, are possible in the mill but seem inconceivable elsewhere. What is most interesting in the steelworker stories are the unexpected moments where real people make vital sense out of the intersections of gender, class, race, and sexuality. From an outsider's standpoint, this "sense" might not "make sense," but for the steelworkers, it is what works and how they choose to live their lives.

For example, steelworkers smoke. Not all of them, of course, but it's a very common habit among them. Traditionally, they open packs on the bottom to avoid touching the filters with their dirty fingers. One person I interviewed smoked constantly while describing his partner's painful and early death from lung cancer. When I expressed surprise, he responded that if you're exposed to the volume of airborne chemicals and other workplace hazards that he breathes every day, why not smoke? It, at least, is enjoyable, and permits you some measure of control.

When steelworkers discuss their jobs, they typically give two iconic general statements: *"It's a man's world,"* and "It's a good meal ticket at the price of ten years off your life" (*The Heat* 151). My interviews reveal that an incredible level of violence toward and harassment of queers is part of the basic steel work environment. To understand how and why, we need to start with a clearer picture of what the jobs are, what the work environment is like, and how the space, the technology, the geography, and the traditions of basic steel production shape the genders and sexualities of those who work there.

When the mills began to lay off workers in droves (starting in the 1980s), one concession the unions wrung from management was that retraining be funded, and funded well. Starting in 1989, for every hour worked, the USW collected fifteen cents, which it used to build and staff schools that current and former steelworkers could attend at no charge. The classes at the resulting Institutes for Career Development were very wide ranging and often involved technology, green industry, or other "growth" fields (http://www.USW.org/resources/training/other). At one of these schools, Jimmy Santiago Baca, an award-winning poet who leads writing workshops with incarcerated people and others, ran a popular class on creative writing and poetry. His goal was to record a dying way of life, in the voices of the people who had lived it. His classes in the mill led to a book called *The Heat*, in which steelworkers recorded their lives and legends.

In one of the stories recorded in *The Heat*, Gary Markley describes his work environment: "Everything about that place scared me. The noises were unbearable. The floor was slick as ice. Hundreds of vehicles and machines were banging, clanking, beeping, crunching, whistling, humming, and screeching. There were sparks of electricity and machinery spinning so fast it made me dizzy. The welding area where two steel coils got joined threw large amounts of sparks in the air" (149). Another wrote about the continuous galvanize line he worked on. "Each galvanize line has a gas furnace approximately the length of a city block through which a strip of steel is run. The furnace is heated to over 1800 degrees to burn impurities off the steel as it moves through the furnace . . . As the heated strip of steel exits the pot, it is coated with the hot zinc. The strip then runs up into a cooling tower, . . . [and then] proceeds down to the basement through what is called a loop car. The coated strip eventually finds its way to the receiving section where it is wound into a steel coil and shipped to a satisfied customer" (122). This worker, Joe E. Gutierrez, describes the "dancing silver dust" this process generated, which he and his co-workers noticed when beams of sunlight came through cracks in the west wall. They "fought to work in that section," enjoying the "little bit of magic" it provided. The dust was asbestos, and anyone who worked there for more than a few years has tested positive for mesothelioma. The union eliminated the asbestos pads, and mechanization eliminated most of the galvanize strip jobs. Asbestos eliminated most of the workers.

Gary: A City Defined by Steel

Steel mills dominate Gary, with U.S. Steel in the center and the ArcelorMittal mills to the east and west. Though they all are still operational, Gary has undergone radical change since about 1960. What was once a bustling industrial town is now a bankrupt, last-choice slum. Gary was recently the murder capital of the United States. When Indiana designates Section 8 subsidized housing in order to comply with federal laws, it does so disproportionately in Gary, thus increasing the concentration of poverty there that followed the mill closings and layoffs. Businesses don't tend to locate in areas where people have little money to spend, which means retail and food service jobs are rare. This urban cycle of poverty occurs in pockets all over the United States, but Gary is often used to represent the larger picture. Gary is such a potent symbol of rust-belt urban decay because the steel mills' ongoing, imposing physical presence there recalls a powerful past that's now gone and because in Gary this urban decay so visibly falls along racial lines.

Gary operates, then, as a powerful symbol of American failure—failure to compete in the global industrial marketplace, failure to find racial harmony, failure to protect the environment. Since the steel industry and Gary had once represented American growth and possibility, with each employee having ready access to union protection and unlimited consumer goods, the contrast with the present reality is especially bitter. In Gary's heyday, churches had grand, vaulted ceilings supported by wooden buttresses. Now, the pews and supports have been burned by homeless squatters seeking warmth. Walking into these buildings, you can almost feel the loss.

To understand how the steel mills affect Gary and its environs, one needs some sense of what goes on in them, and how what goes on has changed. Olshana personalizes the steelmaking process I described earlier by comparing it to cooking: *"You get three raw elements, coal, iron ore, and limestone . . . shipped in. Railroad car loads full of coal, which gets baked at the coke plant until it becomes coke. And then iron ore from Minnesota or other places comes in on barges, and limestone. Well, anyway, these ingredients basically just get cooked. The iron gets melted out of the iron ore and gets poured into big molds. It's sort of like baking. I described it to someone sometime that it's basically like making cookies. 'Cause you get the three basic elements and then mix them together, cooked, iron gets melted out of the iron ore and poured into moulds. After it gets hardened it's called pig iron, [imperfections] get taken off, and these big solid pieces of iron called billets come out, and they get moved around the mill, and then they get melted down and reshaped into whatever it is that production needs. After that, it's just a question of scale. The billets get moved around on railroad cars, and then they get heated up again wherever they're going to be rolled out, or stamped out."*

Early in Gary's history, mills generated the heat for this process by burning coal. The transportation and combustion of coal are both very dirty processes. Dust and smoke leave the air and everything it touches gray and sooty, almost as in Charles Dickens's London. Though coal is cheap and plentiful, it's hard to get enough heat consistently by using it, so as the basic oxygen furnace and continuous casting became common in the mills, there was also a transition to electric firing. Throughout this shift, the cooking process—what is done with the heat—remained fairly consistent.

Most mills have two main components, often called the hot side and the cold side. The hot side is where the steel is cooked, melted, and poured. It

City Methodist Church, Gary, 2013. Photograph by Riva Lehrer.

often contains the coke ovens, and it houses the hardest, hottest, and most dangerous work. This side is where the lowest-paid jobs are located, and the most minority workers. As Wanda says, *"The stereotype back in the day was all the blacks got hired to the east side coke plant. It's very dangerous, it's very dirty, and it's a eight-year contract. You cannot leave from there for eight years, you gotta sign a contract. And a lot of people—there are other races that work there too, but majority of blacks that work in the mill is on the east side. Like when I got hired, and I went to the plant, and the old-timers, the ladies that been there, said you were lucky. 'Cause usually you go here or you go to the tin mill, and the tin mill's on the west side, and people have said the tin mill is like a fraction of the coke plant. People on the east side don't make as much money as people on the west side. They have to work almost a double every day to bring home the 80-hour paycheck that we can bring home. And I don't know why 'cause it's like they actually cook the steel—they actually make it—and it's more dangerous over there, and I don't understand that."*

The other side, often called the finishing mill or the cold side, involves pressing, coating, machining, etc. Steel billets come in and get processed in any number of ways before they leave the mill. Some jobs are hot, and many are loud or involve chemical solutions. This side typically has huge amounts of storage, and various types of equipment, stretching over many acres. One way the steel industry tried to save itself as it foundered in the 1980s was to switch to mini-mills, in which electric arc furnaces enabled a given mill to specialize in one type of output (nails, for example) and thus be able to produce that product cheaper and faster. Often, these mills used recycled metal rather than cooking the steel "from scratch." As long as a steel mill has a melter (a hot side) it counts as a basic steel producer. These mini-mills were mini only in comparison—they covered many acres, though fewer than the region's five biggest mills. They were, in some cases, more successful at turning a profit, at least until the large steel mills adopted some of their strategies, such as incorporating scrap (Hall 23–25). The big mills can work more quickly by, for example, efficiently testing scrap for radioactivity, a small portion of which can contaminate the whole cast, or even the furnace itself.

Steelworkers, once hired, will make a bid for better jobs as they get trained and become eligible. The hot and cold sides constitute one rough division, but there are countless other subsets: rolling, pickling, and blooming mills, for example. And there are countless jobs constructing and maintaining the huge operation that is the mill. A mill is effectively a small city. It needs fire and medical service, electrical and plumbing repair, dockworkers, train switchers, and cafeteria workers. Increasingly, steel mills contract out many of these jobs, which had previously been done by mill personnel.

Knowing what the steel mills do and how they do it helps explain what went wrong starting in the 1980s—why there were mass layoffs and the entire industry contracted. Though steel is still made in the region, and though mills still occasionally open up a new basic oxygen furnace, inspiring headlines in the *Northwest Indiana Post-Tribune* like "Markets Remain Strong as Steel" (June 21, 2006), the number of career steelworkers has declined sharply, as has the standard of living of those who remain. Some people blame the unions, which allegedly forced the mills to hire more and more people at higher and higher wages to do less and less work. When the union won a thirteen-week paid vacation for some workers, that perceived excess became a potent symbol of this trend. Some blame the federal government for its policy that lowered tariffs on imported raw materials as a way to combat inflation, thus allowing countries that subsidize their industries to compete unfairly, or for tightening Environmental Protection Agency and safety regulations that took the focus off profits. Some blame mill management, which continued to build huge mills without including new technology such as continuous casting, requiring them to retrofit even the newer mills in order to be competitive.

The truth probably lies in some combination of all these factors, but whatever the cause, steelworkers feel palpable bitterness and insecurity. People who had given their entire lives to the mill were left with no prospects. Whole communities and regions were devastated. As Chris says, *"You can roll a bowling ball down Main Street in East Chicago and not hit anything. Not long ago, that was a hub of activity."* When I began working in Gary in 2003, the only open businesses on the main drag were fast food joints, payday loan stores, adult book and video stores with private booths, and a storefront called BioBlood Components, which paid people willing to give blood.

How and why this tragic decline occurred is less my focus than how it affected those that remain. No one still working in steel is untouched by these seismic shifts within the industry. And the desperate precariousness of the remaining steelworkers shapes all their behavior, including their reaction to gay people, whose increased visibility in American culture coincided with the decline of the mills and of the Northwest Indiana region. If you live in a ghost town that used to be thriving and you're working on a skeleton crew with no secure future, you are more likely to be insecure and defensive than you are to be flexible and open to change.

Descriptions of specific jobs appear in books such as *The Mill* (Vukmir, 1999), but in the chapters that follow I have left it to the steelworkers to describe their job tasks and everyday lives as they tell their stories. Shifting between jobs is very common. During the course of a career, steelworkers may shift between mills, and they often move between different sections as they come back from layoffs and get slotted into the first available job. Even during the course of one day, a worker might do a scheduled shift at his or her usual worksite and then do overtime in the general labor pool. All this jumping around means that specific tasks or training influences workers' lives less than does the mobile work climate. As Lupe, who has worked only this one job since leaving college more than twenty-five years ago, puts it, *"In working at that one place, I've had four different employers, and worked in five or six different departments, and a lot of different jobs. When you work for a place that's like a small city, it's very possible to work ten different jobs and never get a paycheck from somebody different. I've worked in management and supervision of so many different fields, when you consider that we have our own, not only the steelmaking facility, but also the support stuff, electricity and power generation, steam generation, the transportation of all the semi-finished products, raw materials. Logistics. All the maintenance of different areas.*" Variety is pretty much the only constant.

Working conditions also vary considerably, but they are usually intense. During one heat wave in 2011 when temperatures in Chicago neared 100°, a steelworker posted regular status updates on her Facebook wall as the temperature climbed in her mill, reaching a peak of 122° at mid-afternoon. And the work is not sedentary; workers need to move around and often exert themselves under these conditions, usually while wearing protective clothing. "Calumet Regional Steelworkers' Tales" gives one worker's impression: "You cannot imagine how dangerous it is until you've been out there. Railroad cars are coming in and out of buildings. Tractors are going all over. Semis are coming out. Steel is heavy. It will smash you like you are nothing. In the tin mill I made metal for cans. Handling that product is like picking up a razorblade. Scrap metal is sharp. Fumes are dangerous. The conditions can be sweltering or frigid because, it's 120° in there" (Lane 84).

Fred describes these extremes well: *"My department is so cold. There's nothing between me and the lake on my end of the department, so whatever temperature it is outside, that's the temperature it is in my department. . . . It's cold in there. But it makes up for it in the summer time, where you step out and it's only 90 degrees and you almost faint from the sudden drop in temperature. [The contrast gives you] goose bumps, and you get nauseous, and woozy. I have no idea how hot it actually gets in my department. Those torches that they use to cut through nine inches of steel get to 4,000 degrees, and each burner runs four of those torches at once, and we used to have nine burners, so there's forty-six of those torches and sometimes the slabs have just recently been cast and they're still hot. And sometimes we do what they call hot burns, where they build the slabs, and then they slide the oven up on top of them (that's easier then sliding them into the oven) and they bake 'em up to like 900 degrees and then rush 'em over to our department and we have to walk around on top of them. It's hard to even breathe."*

Fred's tone here is one of boasting more than complaint—he is proud of what he endures, and it adds to the mystique, even the glamour, of the job. Steelworkers often take this tone when describing extreme weather and harsh working conditions, especially when they contribute to the danger of the job. Zach, whom I interviewed during a winter storm, says his plant is dangerous *"especially when the place blows up. They're known for that. . . . It's kind of two different worlds. There's the hot strip and the melt shop, and the melt shop is where they make the scrap into bars, and especially now, they have what's called a wet charge, when there's water, or especially now snow, in the molten steel. Steel and steam don't mix—they blow the roof off. So they do that frequently. A lot of new people are scared. They'll hear a boom that blows the dust off the place. I mean from end to end. You can't not notice it. New people say, 'What was that?' 'It's a wet charge, get used to it.'"* Though there have been numerous fatalities in Zach's mill, the explosions he is describing here are just part of the regular working day, so that only new people are alarmed by the boom. Others just know that it's a wet charge and keep working. And accidents and explosions are just one component of the danger. Though tighter safety and environmental regulations presumably reduce the long-term health effects of working in a mill, Kate maintains that *"it takes life expectancy. Drastically, so they say. In fact, I just lost a male co-worker Friday. Sixty-one years old. Do we know if it would be related to work exactly? I don't know—he was a Vietnam veteran also. But I seen a lot of people that do pass on pretty quick after they retire, where I work."*

I toured the 80" hot strip of the ArcelorMittal mill in East Chicago on June 25, 2011, so I can personally attest that it's big, hot, dirty, and loud. At a hot strip, slabs of steel that have been produced at other locations on site (this is an integrated mill, meaning all the steps happen here) are squeezed into coils of steel. For this to happen, the slabs need to be heated to a cherry red, and then run through a series of rollers. Lots of water is involved for cooling and lubrication. In addition, there are countless fine details concerning the chemical composition of the steel, its thickness, its coating, etc. This plant's customers are mostly automotive and appliance manufacturers, who will order particular amounts of different products, which are then generated from slabs already in storage in the slab yards. There were only a few people moving around the plant floor during this process. Most were sitting up in pulpits, keeping an eye on rows of buttons (all green at the time, thankfully) and many monitors and computer screens. Tools and paperwork coexist in the pulpits. At one point, the workers were trying to solve a problem that had halted production, and they pointed out that the plant was losing $300 per minute. They seemed calm and friendly nonetheless.

They also seemed proud. They took me on a driving tour afterward, pointing out to me the largest blast furnace in North America and the coke ovens. They're proud of their company's safety record, and of their union. I met probably thirty employees total, only one of whom was female and one of whom was Latino. The rest were white males, most between the ages of thirty and sixty. Though I came in on an approved tour with union leaders, we were stopped at the security gate and had to show the guard the email

With my guide on my tour of the 80" hot strip, June 2011. Author photograph.

authorizing our visit. During the driving tour, a patrol car stopped to check on our authorizations.

At times, the mill did feel like a different, wholly alien world. Yet there were familiar aspects as well. Because of Northwest Indiana's unique composition, I passed gambling "boats" and luxury marinas as I entered the mill. More reassuringly, many aspects of the mill resembled the car shop where I once worked, including the gritty, greasy dirt, the heat, and the smell. Drive shafts and hoists look the same, just on a different scale. And I came upon the exact same grease gun that we used in the car shop where I used to work. It had the same ancient black scum all over it. The same two pitted wheels and slimed handle to roll it over to your worksite. The same ancient brass fitting. The same corroded red cloth chord you connect to the air compressor to power it. Artifacts like this grease gun are evidence of the continuity between various manual labor jobs. That kind of continuity is one of the factors that fostered communication between me and the steelworkers I interviewed, making our conversations detailed, intimate, and often surprising.

CHAPTER TWO

Bridging the Divide between Work and Home

A picture, taken by my narrator Phil inside his plant on a typical work day, depicts two hard-hatted men sitting on stools surrounded by heavy equipment, reading. Working in a steel mill typically involves rushing around frantically on deadline and then recording that work on a computer, followed by *lots* of waiting. Increased mechanization and decreased production exaggerates this "hurry up and wait" pattern. Therefore, many steelworkers spend large parts of their day being bored—together. One consequence is that they get to know each other well and come to feel like a family. Another is that they often talk about home life, family, sports, sex, and anything else they can think of in order to pass the time. This nurturing and familial structure, though a valued and important part of mill work culture, has the ironic effect of making it harder for GLBT steelworkers to feel welcome. Nate reflects that *"in the steel mill, guys get very explicit about what's going on in their world, as long as you're not gay."*

In her 1976 pioneering study of white working-class families, Lillian Breslow Rubin observes that one "crucial difference between the lives of professional men and blue-collar men . . . is that the professionals' lives are not so profoundly cleft between work and leisure" (190). While Rubin attributes a "connectedness between the various parts of life" to professional "men" (191), she notices movement in one direction only: friendships, interests, and ideas from the work settings of professionals' lives permeate their leisure time. For Rubin, a professional is someone who brings work home—the workday and its concerns bleed into personal, social time. She wrote in 1976, at a time when a "worker" was understood to be a white male. The issue of who works and how has changed rather dramatically since then, though research like Rubin's that explores the lives of working people as a whole remains scarce. By contrast, for the workers I interviewed, work might not come home, but home definitely does come to work. This chapter examines how issues of personal and home life saturate the steel mill's work culture, and how its presence affects the work, and the workers. Work traditions of gossip, small talk, and cooperation in basic steel mills serve to keep queers invisible, often marginalized and isolated.

In middle-class workplaces, especially those in which nontraditional (female, black, gay, disabled) workers have made inroads, discussion of personal issues is considered inappropriate at work (Rapoport, Rhona, et al. 11–13). If I miss work at the University because my child is sick, my colleagues caution me not to admit that reason, but to come up with one that's less personal (read, less feminine). The effort of working while raising children is not supposed to show in my middle-class workplace. As Rapoport and her co-researchers demonstrate, organizational work cultures continue to be modeled on the industrial models of early capitalism, and they "glorify employees who work as if they had no personal-life needs or responsibilities [and] silence personal concerns" (31). At least in the steel mills, this separation is not an important component of working-class culture. Mill work and family life often overlap. Phil summarizes this well: *"When I leave work, I leave work. I don't so much leave home at home."* Since jobs are typically offered first to family members, many people I interviewed had numerous relatives who worked in the same mill. The workers frequently described going to each other's children's birthday parties, and serving, as Andy observes, *"as your co-workers' therapist."* When Kate described her partner at work, she smiled and relaxed. When I asked whether she liked him, she replied, *"Yeah, when you work with somebody twelve hours, and you're confined to a small space, you learn everything about each other. I mean, I can tell if you're going to the bathroom too many times—what were you drinking last night? I mean, that's why I laugh. It's really comical. I've been real fortunate."* Steelworkers shower together, solve problems together, work in teams for safety and support, and share vast expanses of time together with nothing to do but talk, so they often talk about life outside of work. The schedule of steel mill work certainly doesn't make it easy to have and raise children, or to "have a life" at all, yet both male and female workers are expected to make private, family concerns a central part of work culture and conversation.

For gay and lesbian steelworkers, this integration of the personal into the work setting brings stress. Research by M. V. Lee Badgett and Mary C. King on how and why gay people choose their jobs concludes that many "will attempt to minimize the impact of anti-gay discrimination in their work lives" by avoiding jobs where it is "difficult to pass as heterosexual." Such jobs include ones "that involve high levels of social interaction" (75). According to my narrators, the steel mill is one such workplace.

Erin describes how this environment encouraged her to hide, and thus further withdraw from her work culture. *"One of the things about the mill is that there's a lot of time to talk, so people talk all day long. Depending on what job you're on, you're sitting around in a shanty. You're sitting around in a pulpit. And you could be running equipment, you could be going in and out, but people are talking all day long. Or if you're a laborer you're working beside people and a lot of times hanging out with your shovels talking, so it's very challenging hanging out with people, all night long sometimes, because you're working all kinds of shifts and to hide portions of your life. It's really tiring."*

Erin, who describes herself as *"very interested in people"* and generally eager to hear their stories, recalls particular difficulty when she is unwilling to reciprocate and tell her own. *"This one woman, one day in the locker room, started asking me questions and I wouldn't answer and she got really mad at me,"* Erin reported. *"She said, 'You want to know all about everyone else, but you don't say a thing.' Really, it's like a punch in the stomach. I was so in the closet that I couldn't even tell her about the real, important parts of my life. I was really, really afraid to do that."* If workers are worried about what they might reveal, they're likely to be silent or to keep the conversation superficial. Though less dangerous, this strategy keeps gay and lesbian workers just as isolated as outright exclusion would.

A Chicago-area union activist confided to me that she had been friends with a lesbian steelworker, who had since died. They originally met at the Mesabi Iron Range in Minnesota. When a 1974 consent decree resulted in an agreement between labor and the government requiring the range to hire more women and minorities, it became clear that northern Minnesota lacked racial minorities, and that most straight women were unwilling to relocate to a remote, rural location. Consequently, a large lesbian community developed there, featuring softball leagues, visiting musicians, and endless house parties. Even lesbians who didn't work in the mines would visit this community. When the mines laid off workers, my contact moved to Chicago, got a college degree, and became active in the teachers' union.

In the meantime, Alice Puerala, her friend, began working for U.S. Steel, where she ultimately got elected to high union office. When I asked my local sources about Puerala, they told me stories about her life and her union achievements, but they denied that she was a lesbian—though one acknowledged that she had lived with another woman for many years. There's an existing, transcribed oral history of Puerala, taken in Chicago on September 30, 1977, by Elizabeth Balanoff, who did a series of steelworker oral histories under the auspices of Roosevelt University. In this account, Puerala doesn't discuss sexuality—it never comes up. Yet if you're looking for it, it's there, in comments like: "And I was living with another

Alice Puerala picketing USWA headquarters in Pittsburgh, ca. 1979–82.
Courtesy of the Calumet Regional Archives.

gal so the rent wasn't so bad" or in her response to the question "Tell me a
little bit about your husband or your marriage," to which Puerala responds:
"Well, it was very brief." Puerala was elected to the grievance committee in
1976, and served as union president twice, elected in 1979 and again in 1985
(Warren). What amazes me is that people who worked closely with her for
years didn't know she was gay. Janis observes that Puerala *"was more out
about it early on, but then she got married, and got more political in the union,
and it became a kind of quiet thing."* I've spoken to a lesbian union activist
who felt as if she was the only lesbian doing mill work. She worked, at least
occasionally, with Puerala. If either had disclosed her lesbianism, their lives
could have been less lonely, and less fearful. But evidently, despite the fact
that they communicated extensively with co-workers, neither felt comfortable sharing that bit of information, meaning that they monitored all their
conversations carefully.

Often, steelworkers perfect the skill of talking without saying anything
in order to fit into a workplace culture of disclosure while maintaining secrecy. For example, Gail can tell endless, jovial stories without revealing her
sexuality, or any other personal information. And Athena reflects that *"you
spend a lot of time down, depending on what your job is, in the mill. . . . People*

read, people do watch movies, they do a lot of things they're not supposed to do. Depending what your job is. Like in the mobile tractors, a group of us will go hang out in a shanty, read or talk or sit around and drink coffee. One guy may choose to go sit in his tractor that whole time and listen to the radio in the tractor, and not socialize or participate. Those things happen, they have their little hiding places or whatever. You spend a lot of time there. You do a lot of twelve-hour turns. Guys have historically done a lot of sixteen-hour turns. We probably have some of the best set-up kitchens in the area. . . . We have microwaves, we have crock pots. The electricians have created us things. Grills and stuff. Does management know we have all this?—yes they do. But as long as you get the job done, and you keep things running. . . . But yeah, it's funny 'cause you can see nobody on the floor, and all of a sudden there'll be a cobble [a projectile of molten steel accidentally emitted into the workplace during the cutting process] at the hot mill and suddenly there are people all over the floor. Where did they come from? The company would like you to have busy work during all of that time. There is some stuff you could be doing, but not constantly." All this down time, the conversation, and the cooking, create community, which is an aspect of the work that my narrators value highly, even though their participation is predicated on secrecy. Athena adds: "*If it's hidden, who cares? No, that whole toughness, good ol' boy, I've gotta fit in. That's got to be hard on gay men. I'm sure there are more gay men out there than we know, and I'm guessing they put on a heck of a persona when they're in the mill.*"

Being gay thus forecloses the opportunity for meaningful connectedness at work. Marie reports that she had nothing in common with her co-workers, yet, "*I had a little group of friends from my work area, and I felt comfortable going out with them to the bar drinking—whenever it was, no matter what shift it was. I think part of it was just because I didn't have much else in my life, y'know, I worked, so I think if I was going to have a social life other than sit in front of the television by myself, so that's what I did.*" Though they spent social time together, she describes this as more from convenience than anything else, and Marie never revealed personal information. The need to hide her private life prevented any sense of community from developing.

Though Jay, possibly even further isolated as a gay *man*, has often worked in group settings, and describes the constant homophobic banter and jokes that then filled his days, he now works alone up in a pulpit. Still, he's a personable guy, and people drop by to pass the time, and "*it's usually about really nonsense stuff, but like they'll make faggot gestures, tell faggot jokes, talk about getting their dicks sucked, and bend over. This one black guy teases me all the time about being gay for a joke, and I say, 'Come on, once you have black you never go back.' There are guys out there I totally fantasize about like crazy. But they're the type of guys they're so straight, they're liter- ally homophobic."* Here, conversation isn't about sharing experiences, as in Erin's story, but about power plays and teasing. Jay says it's nonstop, constant insults. *"And they'll say, 'Hey come on, why don't you give me a blow job, why don't you come suck my dick, bitch.' And I'm like, 'Drop your pants, let's go,' and they're like, 'Fuck you.' Or they say, 'Bend over, I'll give you what I've got,' and I'm like, 'OK, come over, I'm ready.' I go, 'You know me, I'd love to get you some place, take your pants down, and we'll go to town.' And they think I'm joking. I haven't lied to them one time, you know the thing of it is, if they ever, ever, ever find out I'm gay, I've always said I was, they just don't believe me. And this is all the time."* Jay admits to being gay ironically—with an exaggeration that insists otherwise—and he's terrified (*"ever, ever, ever"*) that his actual, lived gayness might someday be revealed. Queer workers deploy individual strategies to remove their real thoughts, their real self, from their interactions at work. Day after day, year after year, this becomes both dehumanizing and exhausting.

Sometimes, unwillingness to participate in personal conversation be- comes a problem in itself. Early in his career, Ben held himself at a distance from workplace conversations, trying to keep work life and personal life separate. *"They don't ask me [about being gay] because of the simple fact that, one, I'm not very feminine and not very out there like that. I tend to be a very normal, just run-of-the mill kind of person. I tend to keep to myself a lot. [And, two,] I don't talk about my personal life and I don't want to hear your personal life. I mean if you're fighting with your wife and you need someone to talk to, fine, I guess if it has to be me, and you can't talk to her, I guess. But it's not like if I'm fighting with my partner I'm going to talk to you about a goddamned thing. You're probably going to be the last person to ever find out."*

But this reticence got Ben into trouble as well. *"People ask, 'Do you get treated different because you're gay?' Well, most people don't know that I am, but I get treated different because I'm not nice to people. I don't sit and chitchat. I actually had a discussion with my boss, who yelled at me for not bullshitting with my employees. I'm like, dude, so you're actually telling me, where in our rule book it says that we're not supposed to sit around and chitchat and not have personal conversations, and we're allowed to talk about work, and work only, well you're telling me otherwise, that I have to do that? I didn't know I was required to do that. Well, hell, I'll take two hours and sit and do that. I did it for a while before I stopped. And I'd sit and listen to them gay-bash so many fucking people, it pissed me off. Not to the point that I'm going to come out and get ridiculed, like an idiot, but I didn't want to hear it anymore. And it changed my opinion about a lot of fuckin' people."* Ben here makes the link explicit: to hide being gay, he acts *"not nice,"* and the company reprimands him for the substitution, just as they would have for the act that it conceals. Thus, being openly gay is discouraged, but taking steps to hide it is punished as well.

Work cultures that are hyper-heterosexual and harmful to queer employees occur in all walks of life. What's different in the steel mills is the response, both informal and official, when problems arise. Interesting contrast comes from the study of queer Harvard MBAs done by Annette Friskopp and Sharon Silverstein. They note that some workplaces foster "constant talk about heterosexual sex or dating" and that workers in almost every setting "tolerate jokes and comments based on an assumption of shared heterosexuality, which adds to [queer workers'] feeling of isolation and alienation" (128). However, in response to complaints, many large companies, including IBM, have instituted policies that "make personal conversations off-limits" (129). This is one way to reduce actual or alleged sexual harassment, and it purportedly encourages people to focus on their work. In contrast, as Ben reports, though mills officially frown on *"chitchat"* they sometimes explicitly encourage it as well. Personal conversations are an integral part of the workday, and social exchanges after work are almost obligatory. You don't need to do these things to get a job in the mill, but you certainly need to do them if you hope to keep that job once you've got it.

Andy knew a woman who didn't survive the first round of layoffs at his mill because *"she did her job, she worked her job, she came in, as I always put it, 'She did her eight and hit the gate.'"* He suggests that she was laid off so soon because she was a lesbian, but another cause could be her uncommunicativeness, itself caused by her need for secrecy. It was a damned-if-you-do, damned-if-you-don't situation.

Chris describes an atmosphere of incessant gossip between workers. *"If the place made as much metal as they made rumors, we'd all be millionaires,"* he quipped. *"That's the way it is. Word gets out, and people make assumptions as well. No boyfriend, no pictures on the locker. That kind of thing. There's a lot of guys got pictures of girlfriends, whatnot, on the locker. But a lot of guys don't have anything. I had a couple guys that say, 'hey, he's not married, [Chris], go out with him.' Then the other guy starts blushing. There's a lot of guys scared to death of me. I feel sorry for them, 'cause they're just going to be closet cases all their lives. Frustrated. They're not going to have any outlet of any kind 'cause they're not going to know how to find groups to hang with."* He concludes that *"the fact is we all have to work together and we spend more time together than we do with our families back home."* This high volume of contact creates intimacy, but that's not the same as acceptance. Whether these blushing men are gay or not is not the point; that their personal and dating lives are the source of constant analysis at work makes them nervous about being labeled as queer. Everyone, gay or straight, lives in fear.

Hugo observes that the danger of the work creates a camaraderie in the mill. His work crew spent a lot of time in the lunch room, where they all spent alternating half-hours cooling off from the work floor. He seems almost reluctant to describe their conversation, prefacing this discussion with disclaimers like *"I have to be honest"* and *"I have to admit."* But then he comes out with it: *"Perhaps stereotypically, they talk a lot about women. So I guess if you're a gay man, what would you talk about, well you'd talk about women, I guess because what else would you do? And you can't do the 'down the middle and don't actually say anything' because you're supposed to be their buddy. So basically it was about fucking and getting drunk. I hate to say it, but they weren't talking about politics. It was really rough talk."* Hugo is probably reluctant to confirm this sexist, macho stereotype about working-class men. And the stereotype, which pervades Hugo's memory, relies on exclusions, both of gay men and of *"ethnics,"* who were not welcome in these conversations.

In a workplace built around creating community, even if only through shared insults and jokes, Gail creates safe space by being indirect and "one of the boys." When she got her first promotion in the mill, after shoveling iron ore pellets and cinder up onto conveyor belts for about six months, she became a subforeman in a labor gang. There, she worked with a foreman who came from the same part of Pennsylvania that she did, which gave them common ground. Yet, in years of constant conversation, and even though he knew her partner as well, they never broke out of *"guy mode"* enough for her to reveal any personal information, let alone her sexuality. Athena confirms this pattern, adding that, though there are 3,800 people in her plant, she only knows the *"thirty-six guys that are in my unit,"* because they work closely together, but especially because they go to bars, strip clubs, and Chicago Bears games together. Athena doesn't bring her partner along, reporting that her partner doesn't like sports, or the testosterone-charged atmosphere of these outings. But Athena does, and it is this sense of community—the people in her unit by whom she feels accepted and welcome—that leads her to summarize: *"I like the work. I don't know why. It's great, it's awful."*

Northwest expansion of Inland Steel, Indiana Harbor Works, East Chicago, 1980.
Courtesy of the Calumet Regional Archives.

Athena's comment is not rare—many of the steelworkers I spoke to fit well into mill culture and like their jobs and the money they earn. They regret not being able to bring their real, personal lives into work because they like their co-workers and want to find acceptance with them. Walshoks's study of blue-collar women asks why some women persist in the work even though all are harassed. She concludes that the workers who endured "had a sympathetic feeling for the attitudes and lifestyles of their co-workers" (193). When they were harassed, they interpreted the behavior "with an understanding of the social and economic position and pressures of blue-collar life" (194). My narrators similarly understand that the personal questions are asked to create bonds and to fight boredom, and this system makes perfect sense to them. It just happens to exclude them as well.

This allegiance to mill culture lends irony to the steelworkers' descriptions of chitchat at work. When Erin reports that her colleague's irritation that she always asks questions but never shares her own story feels like *"a punch in the stomach,"* she's registering rejection by a culture to which she wants to belong. She doesn't want to just *"do her eight and hit the gate"*—she wants instead to discuss her life with the people who will most understand the struggles and triumphs of being female in this macho world, of raising a child while subject to erratic shift work, of sustaining a relationship through stress and hard times. Yet fear of rejection and censure by that culture prevents her from fully participating in it—she is forever on the fringes of something she really values.

After describing a grim, even hellish job, Keith reflects, *"But I really enjoy the work."* Surprised, I ask why, and he responds: *"I guess really it's the guys I work with. I'm sure that if I didn't like the guys I was working with, I would hate the job too. They're like a family. And really, you're with them more than you're with your family. It's a very friendly work atmosphere. And I work in a bar, so when we get out, I go over there and open the bar and we all hang out. I like everybody who works there. . . . I get along with everybody. It's a fun place to work."* Though none of these people know Keith is gay, he enjoys their company, and finds them such a pleasure to work and socialize with that his truly awful work becomes enjoyable.

Jay also longs to be accepted by his co-workers, but accepted for who he is rather than for the role he plays. He acts straight at work, ironically by making "gay" comments that are perceived as jokes. This process comes with an emotional cost. *"It hurts my feelings because of how horrible they talk, how graphic they are. It hurts my feelings."* At one point, to mitigate the pain of pretending, Jay got in the habit of creating a persona for himself. Hearing him describe it, I concluded that he sought some control over the pretending—he couldn't change that he was lying, but he could change *how.* *"I used to leave the mill, and I was so stressed out from being in the mill, and there were just so many guys out there that I'd love to have, fantasizing, I'd go to [a bar] out there in Michigan City. I would pretend to be Irish, and I would change my name. I would tell them I was someone else because I didn't want to be me. I would tell them my name was Sean. I just didn't want no one to know who I was, I was afraid. I got so wrapped up in the role that I actually believed it myself. I hated who I was, I hated the lie I had to live, so I . . . made myself into someone else. Well, I was out one night, I went to one of the straight bars, with a bunch of my [work] buddies, we were shooting pool. And I got drunk, and Sean came out. They all went to work and they're making a joke about me being Sean. Thank God the gay stuff didn't come out. But it didn't. But they believed in me being Sean more than they believed in me being [Jay]."* This persona is more likeable, more relaxed, than the "real" persona. Yet, just as for Erin, for Jay there's pathos in his longing to fit in, combined with his conviction that the real Jay would never be welcome.

When gay folks come out in the mills, either voluntarily or involuntarily, there's usually a long period of shaming, harassment, and violence. Some steelworkers, including Bernard and Elise, experience this hostility for the remainder of their careers, but others can use humor and the camaraderie of the mill to gain acceptance. Victor explains, *"I enjoy my life. I enjoy my job, but I've been working so long, and with this heart attack and my back I don't enjoy it anymore. I enjoy the people. . . . Most of 'em have no problem with me. The main boss comes out with a cucumber in his pocket, put it down at his crotch and starts wagging it at me. I say, put that down, Dave, you're not getting near me. But I ain't filing no sexual harassment charges on nobody. We get along, we're family out here, and the few that aren't . . . they aren't grown up yet."*

This relative acceptance derives from a willingness to talk and joke about sex. Victor, who I met at a bar in the smallest town I've ever seen, is a storyteller, a prankster, and someone whose slightly wicked smile would disarm any adversary. As he observes, *"I can be funny about it. Some people take this shit too seriously. Especially when we're on our radios—we're not supposed to do it on the radios, but we do—and I can get the guys just rolling in their trucks."* When I ask for an example, he warms to the subject. *"One guy, friend of mine, he got to asking me, 'Well who's the pitcher and who's the catcher?' I said, well, what's the difference, I'll do either one. I says, what about your old lady, she put the strap-on [on] last night? She the pitcher or she the catcher? He couldn't stop laughing. He couldn't load my semi because he was laughing so hard. Stuff like that. All these guys always talk about their sexual encounters with these girls. So I said, I'm tired of hearing people talk about their sexcapades, you need to hear about one of my stories. One night I picked up a pair of twin cowboys from the rodeo, and they wanted to see the inside of my truck, and so needless to say we slip inside. Well they came up with this thing about cowboy hats and belt buckles. The cowboy hats are fine, the belt buckles are shiny. And that became a long-standing joke out there at the mill, it's still a long-standing joke. Be sure you take a cowboy hat if you're going out with [Victor]. I've been a cowboy my whole life too, line dancing—huge dance floor. It's always been my thing—cowboy hats and shiny belt buckles. They says, 'What's the thing about shiny belt buckles?' I says, 'I want to see my face.'*

As Victor's stories suggest, social interaction and community building are important parts of mill culture. Compared to white- or pink-collar workers, many working-class people spend time together at work. Time waiting. Time shoveling. Time working in pairs or teams to accomplish tasks. There's no public to interact with, no checkout line or office wall distancing you from other workers. Safety considerations typically forbid working alone, and focused concentration is often not required. Sexuality and other personal matters are frequent components of this conversation, as are racial slurs and degrading comments about women, all of which Ben's boss dismissed as *"just mill talk"* when he complained about them.

Phil, who has identified as gay for just a few years though he had his first gay experience as a teenager, describes the tone of conversation in the mill. *"There's this overtone of gay jokes, telling jokes portraying yourself as gay that I hear certain people say, and they use terminology that straight people don't know. One guy made a comment, we were talking about how he was a bear, and I think I was the only person in the room that understood what he meant when he was talking. And then he used the word 'power bottom.' And these are just strange words for somebody who—two years ago I wouldn't have known what a power bottom was if you threw that word at me . . . There's one older guy, if he'll pour you a cup of coffee, he says, 'Nothing's free, I'll take that on trade later,' and then the one guy who we refer to as Bubbles . . . [who] always makes comments about him doing things that are gay. Sometimes it feels like you're standing here alone. When the topic comes up about being gay, or the gay jokes start up, and I look around the room and the entire room's involved in this, then I feel lonely, but most of the time I'm just me. I don't sit and talk to somebody and think about it."* Much of the camaraderie of the mill derives from bringing home life into the workplace, yet this banter excludes queers because it relies on gay-bashing and crass humor.

Kitty Krupat, in *Out At Work: Building a Gay-Labor Alliance*, notes, "What I find most frightening about homophobia is that it's a unifying issue. . . . In a workplace, homophobia can be the one thing many people agree on" (199). Because mill culture creates itself through conversation, just as gay identity invents itself through narrative (Kennedy, "Telling Tales," 345), neither exists outside of language. There can be gay sex, but there can't be gay people without the idea of gay identity. Since the public sphere of the mills consumes the personal in its attempt to ameliorate boredom and build community, and since workers are increasingly diverse and trained (or threatened?) into racial tolerance, their chosen scapegoat for community building is queer folks. Because queer folks are at least potentially invisible, mill culture and workers can pretend they are not present and bond over the commonality that this exclusion creates.

The Showers

Hugo begins his interview with background about his family and the region, and he explains: *"The reason I give you that context is, of course none of that has anything to do with being gay. But the shower room did."* Though showers might seem like a tangential part of mill work, they held a central, recurring place in the stories each male steelworker told me. Since mill work is dirty, and harmful chemicals are often involved, the mill provides shower houses, and even requires that certain workers use them. Harriet was initially hired as a laborer. These are the dirtiest jobs with the lowest pay. *"We swept all day and there would be dust. You'd see women at the end of the day just covered in dust—orange dust from working with the iron, or gray dust from the coke."* These women weren't required to wear respirators, but they were required to shower before leaving the mill. Yet it's not women who tell shower stories. Women are still comparatively rare in the mills, so their shower facilities are uncrowded and private. Not so for the men.

Showers and the men he sees there come up frequently in Jay's description of life in the mills. *"I'd go shower, with those young hot guys, y'know. Oh my Lord, I can't do this, I'm too aroused, they're unbelievable. The one thing about the locker room is if you walk around for any length of time they think you're cruising and they'll tell you that. They all know me a long time out there, none of them think I'm gay, they'll say, 'Oh, no, not him. He's got a lot of women.' And I don't. And I'm in the plate mill, and God really, never ever have I asked anybody at work, but all these really hot guys, it's like being in a candy store, if you're diabetic, and you can't have any candy. It's like you want some, but you can't have it. So these guys are standing there showering and they're making gestures, they're making jokes. Couple of them just come up and grab you and say, 'Now we're getting naked.' I'm standing there, and I'm serious, and I say, 'You shouldn't do that because I'm gay, and I might want you later.' And I'm serious, but they think I'm joking."* The men Jay describes here are not simply showering together for convenience. They know they're in a highly charged, sexualized setting, and they deliberately foster that climate, irrespective of whether they would describe themselves as gay or straight.

When I asked Ben how he identified other gay people at work, he began with a disclaimer: *"You can't even say like, it's all the guys who hang out in the shower house hanging out naked talking. All the old guys do that anyway. It's rather actually disgusting, you know. They can't talk with clothes on. Put something on and then we can talk, even a towel would be nice. I'm a gay man, yes, but I don't want to look at everybody."* Because of the male camaraderie that, in other contexts, would be taken for homoeroticism, established methods for gay identification are obscured and homosexuality itself is harder to recognize. As Chris puts it, *"We were all comrades, y'know, rub each other's shoulders and stuff like that"* which reduces the overt sexuality, and therefore the "gayness" of touching between men. Making these personal exchanges part of run-of-the-mill life co-opts some of the mechanisms for creation of gay identity.

In *Sexual Politics, Sexual Communities*, John D'Emilio concludes that before the Stonewall rebellion of 1969 (the symbolic moment when gay liberation gained enough steam for people to imagine a cohesive gay identity), being queer was viewed as a personal, individual situation. "Most gay men and women discovered their sexuality in relative isolation, and the furtiveness that characterized the gay subculture tended to reinforce the belief that their sexuality was a personal matter. In general, homosexuals and lesbians lacked the experience of belonging to a cohesive social group" (242). This situation began to change as gay and lesbian people interpreted themselves as part of a group subject to systematic oppression. But because the personal (sexual, familial) is interwoven into the culture of mill work, that shift has not occurred for steelworkers.

Most of the steelworkers I interviewed were incredulous that there were other queers in the mills. Erin pointed out that *"it would be cool to meet each other. Maybe before you publish the book, you could have a party and we could all meet. One of the biggest issues is being afraid to talk to each other. When you're in the mill, you're just wondering, is she or isn't she? And you're looking for verbal cues."* Though sexuality and homosexuality are regular subjects of conversation, actual, embodied homosexual people are functionally nonexistent.

Ian started working at the mill right out of high school, and his experience of seeing men there, both working and showering, catalyzed his self-identification as a gay man. *"And what was significant for me, I guess, was I was around lots of men for the first time. I mean, in high school, I lived with my sisters, and my two older brothers had pretty much left the house by the time I was working. I remember in high school, showering after phys ed, and what a nervous experience that was for me, with my developing sexuality, being around lots of naked men, and the teachers. Those memories were impactful on me, and by the time I was at [the mill] I hadn't done phys ed for years, and I remember I was in the showers with all these naked men, and I was like, 'Wow! This is great! What I get to see, a lot of opportunity.' It's kind of embarrassing to say that, but now I knew. That kind of fueled my fantasies and all that. Now I knew."* Ian didn't come out for years, and never at the mill, yet it was the public nature of the mill environment that defined his preferences for himself.

If showering with other men helps gay steelworkers clarify their desires, it also creates anxiety for both gay and straight steelworkers seeking invisibility. Jay remarks that *"I stopped showering out there, because there are so many young guys I'm just afraid I'm going to get a hard-on. It's a normal reaction."* And Ben tells a story about another man who stopped showering at work. *" 'Cause some of the guys that I work with would really probably have an issue. 'Cause there are so many homophobes that I worked with it was unfuckingbelieveable. One of the guys was like, 'button you shirt up all the way 'cause I can't see no other man.' And I was like, 'why, are you afraid another guy's going to be sexy to you or something? . . . I said, 'Where's your locker?' 'In the showerhouse, I don't use it. I don't shower here.' So I'm like, 'you take all the grunge from here and you put it in your car?' I'm like, 'boy, either you're really hiding, or you're a homophobe.'"* The implication here is that because showering happens at work, gay people, or at least gay men, potentially lose their invisibility. And it's that invisibility on which passing for straight depends.

Hugo worked summers as a laborer in a steel mill during college, after which he switched to a corporate job in the mill. His most salient memories are of the shower, *"I remember standing there for eight, ten minutes in front of the guys. And I remember wondering what this was going to feel like—both them looking at me, and me looking at them. And what I mean by that is, I had never been around thirty naked guys, steelworkers, I mean, y'know a lot of these guys were quite fit and they were, traditionally speaking, kind of sexy. And not only that, all the summer students were there, so there were kids my age, and some of them were really good looking, I thought. One time, I don't remember why it happened, whether I happened to be working a double shift, or whether I had to go home. I don't remember. What I do remember is I was the last person in the shower room, and the guy who cleaned the place came in, 'cause he was supposed to clean. And he came in and he stood there, like this kind of <puts his hands on his hips and raises his eyebrows>. And I wasn't used to that. Here I am naked standing there. Of course I knew what he was communicating. And I wanted it. But of course number one I was too young to figure out what to do, and to be perfectly honest, even then I knew he wasn't my type. But apparently I was his. <chuckles>. Which was fine, and y'know I didn't freak out or something, but I said something, 'Hot day,' or whatever, and kind of walked away and got dressed. But at any rate, I thought that's kind of interesting. At work. The situation such that people are naked all the time, um, or they're sweating, I mean it depends on the kind of thing you're into. But if that's a turn-on for you, it's an amazing place, 'cause these guys are all in these, as they now call them, wife beater t-shirts, with muscles 'cause they're hauling steel all the time."* Men in showers—steelworking men in showers—open up possibilities for pleasure that, though forbidden, are nonetheless powerfully there.

When Jerry Davich's article about the research for this book was posted on the *Northwest Indiana Post-Tribune*'s website on January 24, 2010, readers left a rash of comments echoing these concerns, and inexorably returning to the topic of men in showers. One reader has a relative who has worked at USX for over forty years, and "he and his fellow iron workers expressed verbally and sometimes physically, on a frequent basis, hatred towards homosexuals." One steelworker disagrees with this common response, noting "I could care less who of my co-workers are gay or not gay. As long as they are able to do their job and do it safely that's all that matters to me! We steelworkers are a close-knit family and all want the same thing, to go home at the end of the day! Gay or not!" This acceptance is what launches the shower anxiety: "apparently u don't have to shower with a gay steelworker at the end of your shift, while he stares at you uncomfortably. They wanna be gay fine, but they need their own wash house." The comment thread continues, with some saying this discussion is why this topic should remain off limits, some saying that gay men are not sexually aggressive with men across the board, and some noting that one particular shower incident led to the watcher losing his job. When gay men in the mills comes up as a topic, the showers are right behind. Transgender people, whose presence in mill lore far overshadows their actual presence in the mills, are seen as a shower problem as well. Since showering feels like a private, homey activity, violations of taboo such as gay men, public sex, and gender reassignment cluster around showering when it occurs in a public, employment setting.

When Deborah Rudacille interviewed former employees of Sparrow's Point for a book on that mill and its culture, she often found people who describe mill workers as a family (231, 232). One woman notes that she loves "the people." "As much as they can be very macho and crude at times, I like them. There is a certain honesty, and we all look out for each other. We've been together for thirty-two years. We know each other's families. We know each other's sorrows. We know each other's joys. That is the warmth of the place" (171). The mill workers shared a "unity" (232) derived from the overlap between work and personal life. Confirming this pattern, while I was interviewing Chris, he fielded a phone call from a (presumably straight) co-worker arranging a time to come over later to switch out his IV. Chris was on extended medical leave for a work-related illness, and his co-workers stepped in and supported him with an inspiring degree of intimacy.

Yet these same co-workers don't acknowledge that Chris is gay. While they must "know" on some level (his house looks stereotypically gay, and he shares it with another man) he feels that they don't want to confront it head-on. R. W. Connell studied working-class masculinity in Australia. He observes that, since many blue-collar worksites are single-sex and monotonous, smut, ribaldry, and sex are common there (108). He further identifies "a continuum of homoerotic experience among working-class men in a number of social settings. At the same time we must acknowledge that the experience is silenced, that the public language of the peer group is heterosexual. Moreover, it is seriously homophobic" (109). This sort of continuum preempts homosexuality as an identity, and reinforces it as an ongoing but abhorred practice shared by many. Male-male sex is public, something you do at work, while male-female sex is private, stays home, and is what counts. Though this does constitute a divide between the public and the private, it's not the divide we're used to, in which all sex stays home.

Why, then, are public and private, work and the personal, seen as so separate, especially for working people? Kennedy and Davis note, in their study of lesbians in Buffalo, New York, that in the 1930s and 1940s, "lesbian oppression was such that as lesbians and gays come together to end their isolation and build a public community, they also increased their visibility and therefore the risks of exposure." They handled this increased visibility "by creating as clear a separation between work life and social life as possible" (55). These people maintained two entirely separate identities, and two corresponding wardrobes. As time passed, and Buffalo lesbians became more confident, they sought out jobs that allowed them to preserve their bar identities even while at work. Interestingly, this largely appeared to be an issue of outfits, or of uniforms. The bar crowd cultivated a certain look, while work and family life required adherence to norms of femininity signaled by nylons and a skirt. Freedom, for them, became the ability to wear their butch "uniform" even when they were at home or at work.

There is a long close-up of a woman putting welding gloves into her locker in the documentary video called *Women of Steel*, produced by Beth Destler and Steffi Domike (Domike is a former steelworker and now an organizer for the USW). The video opens with a worker striding toward the camera, only genderless work boots and dirty work pants displayed. When her whole body is revealed, her hard hat, welding gloves, thick coating of dirt, and bold demeanor mark her as primarily a worker, and only secondarily a woman. The first thing she does is strip, shower, and change. She thus becomes a woman, albeit a tough and independent one. The close-up on her locker emphasizes this contrast—singed welding gloves conceal her neat, red fingernails. And the whole sequence offers an insight into the division between work life and personal life in blue-collar culture: you wear different clothes in each.

As a professor, if I wear my work clothes to, say, parent-teacher conferences or a bar, they attract no attention. Not so when I worked as a car mechanic. Once a month or so, I would leave work early to get my daughter to the orthodontist before his office closed. This left me no time to shower or change, though I did wash my hands. Some people tried not to notice, but if my daughter asked me to go into the office with her, the orthodontist typically looked me up and down, making no attempt to conceal his disgust. Occasionally, he asked me what was on my boots. I wish I had remarked that the dirt on my uniform helped pay for the shine on his floor, or that dealing with dirt and grease is not worlds apart from dealing with spit and blood. But mostly I was just irritated by the scorn in which he held my job, and therefore me, and the way that evaluation was made visible by my uniform after a full day's work. The hands and forearms of someone who does manual labor are never completely clean. The smell never really washes off. Not to mention the health hazards, which can never be erased. But when you shower and change, you leave most of both the dirt and the stigma behind. And the effort to leave these behind bolsters the distinction between work and the personal.

As I've suggested above, that same distinction collapses in the other direction, mostly through semi-obligatory workplace conversations. That's what creates the "protective family atmosphere" (Rudacille 232) at the mill. And queer people want to be part of that family: an interest in the work and a comfort with mill culture are what draw people to the work initially, and then enable them to stay on and succeed. Although gay identity can be made invisible, the inclusion of storytelling and public showering in each workday challenge that invisibility. They make it easier to detect and thereby isolate gay people. Often, they cause gay workers to preemptively isolate themselves. Thus, ironically, the inclusion of the personal at work causes greater loneliness and isolation for gay and lesbian workers.

CHAPTER THREE

Secrecy—Its Logic and Consequences

Most of the steelworkers I interviewed are "in the closet" at work. Those who are more open are still acutely aware of whom they tell about their sexuality, and how. This chapter looks at the costs queer steelworkers encounter in keeping their sexuality secret. That there is a cost is not surprising since work is a huge part of most people's lives, affecting how we act, how we perceive ourselves, and what seems possible to us. More pragmatically, work consumes a large portion of our waking lives.

The work setting of the steel mill structures the sexuality of people who work there. Events that happen to steelworkers before they work at the mill, or concurrently with working there but in other locations, affect their attitudes about sexuality and its dangers, their choice of occupations and how they conduct themselves while at work, and their sense of what it means to be gay.

At first, I was surprised by how closeted the steelworkers are. The accepted narrative of gay and lesbian life is one of improvement, in which each succeeding generation, even each new decade, brings more freedom, more openness, and more acceptance. The historian John D'Emilio concludes that between roughly 1980 and 2000, "organization, community, culture, and visibility have translated into real, significant victories against the laws, public policies, and cultural practices that have oppressed us[,] . . . and the bottom line is a new social tapestry. It is not simply that we are different among ourselves, that our community is open and visible. The whole society has changed. The business of daily life in America is different because we are there in an open and visible way" (126, 127). The lived experiences of the steelworkers I interviewed provide a stark contrast to this description of change. Not only their jobs, but also the world in which they move, continue to actively, rigorously oppose homosexuality.

Gradually, after talking to many people in Northwest Indiana and the steel industry, and after interviewing many steelworkers, I began to get a clearer picture of why these people stay in their steel closets. One example is Danielle, who *"was sexually abused as a child by a caretaker, not a parent, by a caretaker. That person said, 'you want to be a girl, well this is how guys* treat girls.' Man, I learned a lot real quick." The caretaker and others taught her this lesson regularly and repeatedly over the next ten years. Danielle is proud that even being repeatedly raped as a child didn't shake her confidence about her true identity. *"But I don't think that was very formative on me. It didn't change who I was. It didn't stop me, and I think that was the person's intentional goal, and it didn't work. Dealing with that made it easier to deal with everything else. Being six years old and having sex already, then being an adult and having people laugh at you is not the same thing. But I didn't stop. I got nailed by that person several times 'cause they kept catching me. Only when I was dressed as a girl did it happen. I didn't like it, but I wasn't going to stop being who I was. So."* She came out at work after she had her second heart attack, concluding that the stress of hiding was as likely to kill her as the violence she anticipated if she stopped. She also felt that the early rape she'd been victim to provided her a sick kind of immunity from new trauma. The jury's still out on that.

Elise, who started working at U.S. Steel's Gary Works in 1967 while presenting as a man, decided, in 1994, to extend her weeklong vacation to two weeks, after which she returned to work presenting as a woman. The death threats and the damage to her locker and her car were immediate and intense. Soon the plant assigned her a bodyguard, who would meet her at her car and escort her to her jobsite. But that still left the whole shift, during which the standard reaction was, *"If you're going to be a woman you have to learn to suck dick."* This education was not, she states, optional. *"So they would take their stuff out of their pants, grabbing ahold of me, when those people were not supposed to be in the control room. There was physical violence, too, not just to mention that."*

These rapes occurred between 1980 and 2000, the period during which D'Emilio identifies a real change in the lives of queer folks and of mainstream society. For our culture as a whole, his claim is accurate and insightful, but for the steelworkers, the world got less rather than more accepting of gayness during those decades. Violence and harassment didn't happen just to transgender people, or just to queers who came out, or only to those who stayed hidden, but to everybody. Antigay violence and rape affected men, women, bisexuals, white people, black people, and Latinas, as well as those who courted attention and those who scrupulously avoided it. Even one narrator who asserted that he faced no discrimination at work because he had managed, over the years, to face it all down and get people to accept him as he is showed me, on his cell phone, a picture of workplace graffiti saying, "DIE FAG DIE."

There is no safe way to be gay in the mills. There has been little to no improvement in that situation. All gay folks, and those like some transsexuals whom the mill environment identifies as gay even though they themselves don't, can be physically, brutally punished at any time. Many have been, and the others live with the daily possibility. Even Larry, who I thought would have an easier time since he lives in the more tolerant environment of Canada, reports that *"at work I got ridiculed. Insults on every bathroom wall. I learned to control myself, and not let it bother me. I didn't care. It went on for, I'm not kidding, twenty-five years, I mean really bad stuff. People wouldn't want to work with me. And at the end of the day, we had showers. I mean, we would go to work, change from our street clothes, and then at the end of the day we were supposed to shower. A lot of them, if I walked in they'd freak out, yelling 'Fucking faggot.'"* Even those who feel physically safe often report feeling emotionally vulnerable. Norman observes that working with people who hate you, even if they don't know it's you they hate, feels like *"walking a tight rope"* every hour of every day.

When Harriet was sixteen years old, her father caught her in bed with a girl. He reacted angrily and decided to send her to relatives in Texas to prevent any further such exploits. So, she says, *"I ran away. I was young, alone, living in my car. I moved in with a gay friend, but then he died. It was the 80s. Sleeping in my car was not uncommon. I was seventeen, scared, lonely, no money, uneducated, abandoned. You grow up pretty fast. I got a job at a pizza place where my girlfriend worked, and I was pretty open there. I figured 'what do I have to lose?' I had no home and no family already.*

"My girlfriend was popular and feminine, and the people that hung out there didn't like me dating her. I was brutally raped at age seventeen. Just like in Boys Don't Cry. They wanted to show me what a woman was for. What a man could do. They made me pay. I was a virgin. I almost died. It happened in a junkyard. That kind of showed how they felt about me. It happened in a car, back seat of some huge car. With power locks. I know because I fought to get out. Desperately. Doors wouldn't open. I tried to smash the windows. All the windows. I couldn't get out. But I fought them. My head was all swollen because they beat me with a gun. And I almost died. I was bleeding and I could barely walk. They threw me out of the car like garbage. I was barely dressed.

"But I fought them. I made it as hard as I could. I bit one guy on the hand [she points to the web between her thumb and first finger] and he was bleeding pretty bad. Only two of the four actually raped me. The others gave up because it was too much work. I remember looking up while they were in the act of raping me. I saw the moon. It was a full moon. And I asked God to forgive them

for doing this to me, because I knew I couldn't forgive them. And God blessed me then, because I don't remember the sex act at all. There is a total wall there. And I'm grateful for that. That I don't have to live with that memory. That's how I know there is a God."

Harriet never pressed charges, not wanting her name to appear in the paper, which would expose her family to public shame. Instead, she developed a problem with drugs and alcohol and ultimately enlisted in the Marines, believing its structure might help her recapture control of her environment and her emotions. She also needed the income. When she was involuntarily discharged for homosexuality, she was referred to the mills, which often employ veterans returning from active duty. Though her rape preceded her job at the mill by more than five years, it has colored everything she has done since then, including her mill work. For example, she keeps her personal life very secret at work, having learned what might happen if word gets out. And she is relentlessly conscious of her body, and always on guard. As she says, *"I had to be aware of myself constantly. If I bent over, I had to be sure no one was behind me taking a peek. I didn't let anyone near me who might brush up against me. If my T-shirt got at all wet (which happens—I'm a laborer, remember), I had to go to the bathroom and change it right away. And they deliberately cranked the air conditioner up high— hoping to get a little rise out of me, I guess. Pathetic, but that's the way they thought, so I had to think that way too."* Since her rape, Harriet has chosen jobs that utilize her strength and fulfill her desire to keep herself safe and isolated. *"They thought I wouldn't make it—thought I was just a little Latin woman who wouldn't survive."* But she always does.

A week after I interviewed Bernard, he called me from the hospital to follow up. He explained that his doctor had *"yellow carded"* him (signed an extended medical leave form). His blood pressure wasn't responding to medication, even at ever-increasing dosages, so his doctor discouraged a return to the stress of the mill. Bernard then quipped that this was just as well, since the threats against his life and safety had been escalating, and time away might diffuse the anger. Bernard was first hired by U.S. Steel in 1967, and has been harassed more or less continually ever since then. He has filed claims with the Equal Employment Opportunity Commission (EEOC) and the American Civil Liberties Union but never received any encouragement or support. He reports, *"I applied for assistance with the EEOC and I spoke to a lady named Chrissy and she told me there was no law on the books that protect me as a homosexual. As far as they were concerned I was on my own. I was so despondent I never wrote back."*

Bernard changed his phone number several times during our brief acquaintance, each time in response to death threats and other forms of verbal harassment. He is on medication for anxiety and high blood pressure, and he looks exhausted by the constant fighting. There are moments when I catch a glimpse of what he could be—what he once was—moments when he seems relaxed and genuine. He'll be thinking about the past and telling a story and his voice will get louder and his gestures more expressive. His eyes are more alive. There's a lovely, queeny man sitting before me then, laughing at himself, adapting to new situations, and having a good time.

But these glimpses are brief, and Bernard almost apologizes for them. He returns to being an older man in a stained V-neck sweater, taking prescription bottles from a wrinkled plastic bag. He tells and retells his sad litany of resentment, looking for reassurance that he is not alone and that his experiences mean something. Early in his mill years, Bernard says, coworkers demanded sex from him constantly. *"Those men made my life miserable. There was a few other men that were gay in the mill that was almost at retirement age, that had a reputation. They would have sex with men at the job, in the parking lot. So they thought if you were gay that it was wide open season to do whatever they wanted to do with you. I was not that type of person. If anything, they thought I was arrogant and a snob and a spoiled brat. I was messed with, I was harassed, my car had been tampered with. I was harassed when it came time to change clothes in the shower, in the locker room. Some men would come around you in the nude soliciting themselves in a sexual way to you, asking you to give them oral sex, or asking you to go in the shower and they would penetrate you. It didn't happen all the time, but every now and then that happened. And then you had the other extremes that knew you were gay and it was their life's mission to beat you or hurt you in some kind of way. And then there was another type, and this one guy I'll never forget. . . . He's the kind of a man that I would categorize in the realm of Jeffrey Dahmer, who probably has homosexual gay tendencies, who would probably freak off with you, but once he realize what he does he can't handle it, and then he wants to hurt you. I would run into those type of man in the steel mill as well."*

For Bernard, pride comes from endurance and from a certain cocky self-knowledge. He has paid for his preferences, but at least he acknowledges them. He tells me about a manager who found out he had a Mercedes and then asked to borrow the key. *"His voice got real low and he said: I know Candy. And I smiled to myself, 'cause what he didn't know [was that] I knew him back in the early 70s, because he used to be one of them men that would come over by Broadway to get his penis sucked by transvestites, and Candy was one of the ones that was doing this with this man, and I played right along with him. And he didn't recognize me dressed in men's clothes. If he seen me made up he might recognize me, but not in street clothes, and plus I'm a lot older, heavier then I was then. At that time I was 110 pounds, petite, and I hate to say it, I was a bitch on wheels at that time. He . . . came over to the line with Sal, and asked if I wanted overtime to pay for my Mercedes. I said, 'How come you think that's not paid for? My ex-lover bought me that car just before we broke up. I earned that car with twenty-five years of my life.' They were stunned, because they couldn't imagine a man buying something like that for another man. I know people who have gotten something much more fabulous than a car. I'm not one of 'em and it grieves me."* Though Bernard's loneliness is palpable, he has courage, determination, and a wicked sense of humor on his side. It feels like he has made a choice, more or less consciously, to be himself and to pay whatever price is asked in exchange for that freedom.

In contrast to Bernard, most people I interviewed avoided harassment at work by not getting labeled as queer. They didn't deny it, necessarily. But that's not the point, since Bernard didn't identify as gay at work either— it was just assumed. Most people I interviewed who were harassed (or worse) at work acted in ways considered inappropriate for their gender, which made them appear gay in the mill context. To avoid detection, male steelworkers exaggerate masculinity, and female steelworkers simply avoid personal topics. Lupe notes that very few people in the mill where she has worked for twenty-five years know she is gay. But she adds, *"I shouldn't put it like that. Probably a lot of people know, and just don't say anything about it. Michael Signorile, when he wrote his book on coming out, he said, when people stop asking if you're going to get married, or stop asking if you have a boyfriend, that's a pretty good sign that they know. But, I mean, there's a few people that I've told, and a few more people that have let me know that they know, and that it's OK. I do have a pretty good number of allies."* As long as their sexuality is unstated and not obvious, queer steelworkers can slide in under the radar. The people at the most risk are men with *any* feminine traits, or women with *lots* of masculine ones.

Wanda had problems initially with co-workers saying they couldn't tell if she was male or female. She has a masculine demeanor and style, but, as she says, *"When you're in the steel mill everyone basically looks the same. You have on the greens, or now oranges, and you have on old clothes that you really don't care about. And in the winter you're bulked up. Y'know, lunch time you take your hard hat off, and people just looking."* One person was particularly offended by her lack of femininity. He *"would say things like, 'Y'know, you should try it . . . being with a man.' I would just laugh it off, like I don't know—whatever. It was in '09 we got laid off. By this time I was already in my new department, but all the laid-off people with less time had to go to the tin mill, and it was basically everybody from my old department, including him. And he would make those comments again. One time we were walking, it was me and [another co-worker, Brad] walking with this other individual. And he grabbed me and pulled me into this corner, and he was like, 'you need to try it.' And [Brad] was looking like, 'what the hell, y'know man, come on.'"* Even Wanda's co-worker, whose real name she chose not to reveal, knows that veiled threats of rape are unacceptable, and in this incident, he reminds this *"other individual"* of his presence as a witness.

But the comments did not stop, and Wanda goes on to describe *"another situation—I carry pens in my pocket, a lot of pencils—and that individual wanted to use a pen, and he reached in my pocket, but he went in like this, and he was rubbing my nipple. And I jumped back, and I went right in to Sherry, who was the civil rights chairperson, and we were all co-workers and all friends, and I told her, 'I'm filing charges. Saying something is one thing, but when you put your hands on me and you do that manner, there's a problem.' And [Brad] had saw that, and he was just like, I can't believe he would do that. So I talked to him, that individual, and I told him, 'Y'know what, this is out of line. You will lose your job right now if Sherry was to submit this document to labor relations. And I don't want no one to lose their job, but you need to re-spect me, you need to respect the fact that I'm gay, and you don't need to make comments. You don't need to even say hi to me any more. I don't feel comfort-able around you, you been making these comments for the past six years, I just blow 'em off, but when you touch me today, that was it, 'cause it's like, now, what's the next thing to happen?'*

"And of course now people would believe you, but you don't want to take that backlash that may come with it. At the time, I wasn't scared, 'cause he wasn't like, come here <grabbing gesture> it was like he grabbed me, like you need to come over here and do this, laughing about it. And I'm more like, 'Hey!—who is this person?' After the fact, it did shake me up, 'cause I'm like, what if [Brad] wasn't there? We were—I'm from the sheet division, but we were in the tin mill. I personally am not familiar with that area. I know it's huge. And it has a lot of black spots I would say. No one could hear me. When I think about what could have happened, it does frighten me. It frightens me to a certain extent."

The mills are huge, covering many square miles. They never stop produc-tion, since the heat in the furnaces is cheaper to maintain than to restart, so

The imposing physical presence of steelmaking is exemplified in this
Bethlehem Steel plant, ca. 2000. Photograph by A. K. MacGrew.

someone is always working there, though the top managers generally work
only during the day. Many mills are on the water, cavernously empty, and
old, so a scream, or a body, could be hidden very easily. Lakisha describes
one mechanic working off his task list *"in the far corner of nowhere, as far as
the mill was concerned, and he had a heart attack and he dies, because nobody
knew where he was and nobody saw him back there."* Hours passed before
someone noticed he wasn't at lunch, and by the time they found him he
was dead.

According to Olshana, *"There were so many places in the mill, because it
was so old parts of it, there was a room that guys had set up with psychedelic
posters and stuff. It was dark, and you had to go through some passageways to
get there. I had the feeling that not everyone knew where it was. The walls were
painted black, and it was a little hideout. I think there were cushions, blacklight
posters, it was underneath somewhere hidden away."* So when Wanda notices
"black spots" where she could be dragged off and raped, she's not exaggerating. Because of mechanization, the mills are much less crowded now
than they once were, which leaves ample room for unsupervised activities.

When you combine this environment with the anger and resentment felt by many of the remaining workers, which often targets gay people, you have a very scary situation.

Dave puts it very clearly. *"Again, being gay was not something you wanted to bring out in the mills. I've had a couple people who really wanted to beat my butt. I had to be extremely careful in the showers. I tried my best not to intimidate people. I really wasn't out a whole lot, because, y'know you get afraid."* Even when there isn't overt harassment, there's an atmosphere of constant antagonism. The other workers let gay folks know they aren't welcome, and it gets worse, according to Gail, as you go into the hot mills and the blast furnaces—the sites of the more dangerous and dirty jobs. As Gail explains, *"Any time you have lower education, you have more harassment. . . . They'll mess with your equipment, you go the warming room, and you relax and cool out a little bit, and you go back out and slap your hat on and you got a bunch of grease [that bullies put in your hard hat] coming down your face—stuff like that."*

Maybe the most telling comment is one I often heard when I asked what it was like to be gay and work at the mills; people frequently provided some version of Keith's response: *"I really can't offer an opinion on it because I'm not gay in the mills. As far as they're concerned, I'm straight."* Fear of being ostracized, of harassment and violence, leads many workers to "play it safe" and maintain two entirely separate identities. Fred, who is out at work, describes queer steelworkers' options this way: *"I look at my gay friends who are in the closet and I think they're sniveling little cowards, and then they watch how I get treated, and I can't blame them."*

George Alan Appleby, author of "Ethnographic Study of Gay and Bisexual Working-Class Men in the United States," agrees that most remain hidden as a matter of survival, being very careful about sharing any personal information (57). Thus, most blue-collar workplaces appear to contain few or no queers, since "gender role conformity appeared to be the rule. Those few men who were effeminate, however, pointed out that they had to fight to defend themselves quite often" (62). Yet this research and mine leaves me wondering why. What is it about steel mills that makes their workers so antigay, so resistant to the increased openness to GLBT people that characterizes a widening segment of American culture?

As Allan Bérubé argues, "In the United States today, the dominant image of the typical gay man is a white man who is financially better off than most everyone else" (203). To understand why steel mills are so inhospitable to gay folks, we need to think about why our mental picture of gayness is set in upscale urban locales rather than in plants, remote bars, or trailer parks. Stereotypes and assumptions about what it means to be gay and what it means to be a blue-collar worker—and the overlap, or lack thereof, between these identities—become mutually reinforcing.

For the steelworkers I spoke to, class identity derives less from income than from social factors, and certainly scholars of class and privilege understand this point well. Most of the steelworkers I interviewed make between $60,000 and $100,000 per year. Yet to reach these totals, they work nearly constant overtime, hoping to stockpile earnings since their employment future is so uncertain. Frequent layoffs, high risk, and low status jostle with relatively high hourly wages to create class confusion.

Early in my research, I visited the United Steelworkers' union headquarters in downtown Pittsburgh. I met with Steffi Domike, a former steelworker and current organizer for the union, and with Hillary Chiz, the civil rights coordinator for the union. Both remarked with some surprise that in their vast high-rise building, packed with hundreds of offices containing progressive union staffers, there was not one single out gay person. Chiz also noted that during her tenure and that of her predecessor (whom I also met) there had been no complaints filed by LGBT steelworkers. She was quick to note that this record pointed not to a lack of problems experienced by gay people at work, but rather to a climate so inhospitable to gay people that they were more likely to endure mistreatment or quit their job than they were to complain to their own union (personal interview, Hillary Chiz, 16 April 2010). Chiz's interpretation gains support from research on recent unions' progress "towards the representation and protection of their sexual minority members" (Hunt and Boris 91). As of 2002, the Steelworkers' Union (USW, formerly USWA) still resisted this trend, failing to make five out of the six changes that most American unions had introduced since the 1990s (Hunt and Boris 92). This is not an environment calculated to encourage the submission of grievances by gay or lesbian employees.

Amber Hollibaugh, who describes herself as a "high femme" lesbian activist, writes personally and passionately about the absence of working-class people and perspectives in the mainstream gay movement. Since working-class and blue-collar people and concerns have not been a part of gay activism or politics, many felt they had to choose between sexual and class identification—there was no way to integrate these two identities. Hollibaugh insists that unions are working to change that. She believes this change is possible, and is happening. "At least in my life, if you were a lesbian, the only choice was to be quiet or to leave. In the trailer parks I came out of, man, those were the options. You could be a homosexual and get the shit kicked out of you at work all the time, or you could leave and try to have a life with other gay people. That is no longer true" (235–36). She then points out that most gay people are working-class and that the union movement needs the support of queers of all stripes. Her argument here is utopian and polemical, and she also acknowledges that unions often ostracize, rather than draw from, populations she believes would strengthen them, such as sex workers and people living with AIDS. Further, she notes that queer politics and culture exclude class. "Why? Because those working-class dykes with AIDS were never the dykes that the white, middle-class, identity-oriented lesbians wanted at the table. They never wanted butch/femme dykes with two years of high school to be the people who articulated the political agenda of the social movement" (222). So, if working-class people aren't welcome in the queer community, and queers aren't welcome in blue-collar workplaces, then working-class queers have no place.

Dorothy Allison, another pioneer scholar on queer working-class identity, grew up poor, abused, a lesbian, and a writer, in Greenville, South Carolina. "My sexual identity," she says, "is intimately constructed by my class and regional background, and much of the hatred directed at my sexual preference is class hatred—however much people, feminists in particular, try to pretend that is not a factor" (23). Because of her class background, she says, she is "accustomed to contempt" (24) and has had to learn and relearn how not to direct that contempt at herself. This insight helps explain why queers are so reviled in the mills: working-class people are reviled, often even by themselves, so contempt is part of the work culture, easily applied to gay people. I have already quoted Ben, who remembers: *"I'd sit and listen to them gay-bash so many fucking people, it pissed me off. Not to the point that I'm going to come out and get ridiculed, like an idiot, but I didn't want to hear it anymore."* Here, I want to emphasize that for him, both coming out and staying in foster self-loathing and self-blame.

As gay people's visibility and acceptance have grown, the visibility and status of mill workers have shrunk. Unlike people a generation ago, most folks I spoke to who live in Northwest Indiana don't know any steelworkers and often don't think that there *are* any anymore. In fact, the number of steelworkers in the United States is about a tenth of what it once was, and the region's overall population as well as its population of steelworkers has declined. Many factors contribute to this decline: public support for unions was in decline well before Tea Partiers chimed in, and there has been a shift in expectations that means almost all American children are being encouraged to go to college and pursue a profession. Literally the same decades that brought public pride to gay people brought a decrease in income and status to American industrial workers. One effect of these concurrent shifts is the virulent anti-gay atmosphere in the mills.

Chris describes these changes: *"Back in the 70s and 80s nobody cared, but then the movement came in and put a kibosh on a lot of stuff. People became more aware. The young people they think they have to put on airs to show their masculinity. . . . Back in my disco days, it's like everybody did what they wanted to, if you went into a club, or some gay person went into a club, it was like no big deal nobody cared. Now sometimes it's like you're the enemy or something."* One might argue that there's currently more cultural and social support for being gay than there is for being working-class. As Dorothy Allison and Amber Hollibaugh point out, being poor and working industrial jobs is a legacy one is "supposed" to escape rather than embrace. Those trapped in it tend to scapegoat gays in general and preemptively ensure that no one from their community identifies as gay. In the mills, then, increased social freedom for queers has resulted in a backlash.

Miles describes a coworker who eventually left the mill to become a New York City police officer. Miles believes this person *"got out of there"* because of the mill atmosphere of harassment and hostility. *"He had incidences where people were writing on his locker some nasty . . . pejorative graffiti. And he went in and he says to the guy in HR, 'Somebody wrote on my locker. I expect it removed by the end of my shift, no questions asked.' And it was removed. But he stood up for himself, I liked that. When push came to shove, he wasn't."* There's a grudging respect in how Miles tells this story, especially in the pun at the end. He's proud of his co-worker for fighting and winning, and also for finding more congenial employment. And there is shock value to Miles's and his co-worker's assessment that the New York City police force would provide more acceptance of gay employees than a steel mill.

Uninterrupted lack of acceptance defines the career of Larry, who calls himself a "dresser" and often presents as Lisa. Attacking him united the other workers behind a common goal. He explains: *"I mentioned about me being harassed every day for about the last twenty-five years at [the mill]. And especially at shower time at the end of the day. You see I'd be checking out the guys and once they found out who I was they would be calling me Faggot, Sissy, Pansy, etc. And once they found out I had a boy friend, my first love, I was mugged and beaten up three times. This was in the downtown area when we had five to six gay clubs. It was as if they were waiting for me to come out. I did end up in the hospital on two of those times. Oh and yes I was dressed as Lisa. Then there were times when I was Larry and there would be three or four guys waiting for me in the parking lot. I did my best to defend myself. And yet I would always keep my head up and try and carry on my life the way I wanted to."* Larry refuses to stop "dressing," and to stop searching for love. He thinks it might be easier for him if he surgically or legally changed sex, but he doesn't want to—he likes being a man in a dress (and heels, makeup, the whole deal) and he's not going to let continued, relentless harassment and violence stand in his way.

Stories like Larry's don't get covered by the gay media and don't play a central role in queer politics or activism. As Allan Bérubé claims, the "un-examined investment in whiteness and middle-class identification" of the gay movement leads to "a racialized class divide that continues to tear our nation apart, including our lesbian and gay communities" (204). The instances of outright discrimination I hear about from the steelworkers don't constitute part of GLBT public policy discussions, and that silence is the result of class considerations.

Nate experienced the steel mills' exclusion of gayness personally when his ex-wife revealed to his employers that he was involved with a man, and they fired him. He had recently checked in with them about his job security, and they had assured him that he was at no risk of being laid off. But then they learned he was gay, and he was eliminated immediately. Nate got a job in retail at a home décor chain, *"and I was just having an absolute wonderful time after being closeted in the steel mill, and I'm a very masculine man and all that, but it was just kind of fun to be gay. And I was. Not that I was flamboyant, or wore feathers or boas, or heels for that matter, but I did come out, and I made no bones about the fact of who I was. And I had told [my partner], as soon as I left the steel mill, that I would never deny you again, 'cause at the steel mill, they did realize that someone new was in my life, and they kept saying, 'When do we get to meet her?' And I'd say, 'You'll get to meet my special person sometime.' Or, 'You'll get to meet the love of my life.' I could never say his name, or even indicate his gender, for fear of losing my job. I had to be careful in all my conversations."*

This much hiding—this constant vigilance—takes a great personal toll on the steelworkers. Many people I interviewed are regulars at Alcoholics Anonymous (some referred to this as "Gay A"), and health issues related to stress are commonplace. Danielle observes, *"I'm ten years from retirement, I'm getting up there. Had two open-heart surgeries and three strokes. . . . I think stress had a lot to do with it though. . . . Hiding is a lot more stressful, you're like, 'who's gonna catch me?'"* In an economic analysis of gays and lesbians at work, M. V. Lee Badgett observes that decisions to remain closeted at work "are costly strategies for gay men, reducing the individual's self-esteem, depth of friendships, and loyalty and increasing his stress level" (58). He concludes that, while workers may choose to stay hidden for their own advancement, this decision costs their employers and our society productivity in the long run (70).

When Nate was dismissed after thirty-four years at the mill, he was allowed to walk out independently, without armed escort. *"I did not have that embarrassment. I was able to very proudly walk off with my head held high, and it was a good thing, because the steel mill was not a good place to work, it was dirty, lots of health hazards. And it was hard work, hot, dirty, and it's no place for anybody to work, but it pays well so people were willing to put themselves through those risks. A few years back, we had lead. We use the stuff to temper the wire, and the lead levels of a lot of our guys was just off the charts; they ended up having to wear moon suits to filter the air so they didn't breathe in all that excessive lead. Lots and lots of dangers in the place, besides the fact of burns, fingers getting cut off because of all this fast-moving machinery. It's not a pleasant place to work. And to have to carry the extra burden of not being able to share things that people usually share. 'What are you doing Saturday night?' 'Well, I can't tell you because I'm gay.' There was just a lot of things like that, and we'd have to talk in circles."*

Nate describes tricks he developed that enabled him to communicate with his co-workers and build the bonds that are obviously so important to him, without revealing the things he considered real and important about himself. *"I was very good at embellishing my stories in a heterosexual way. That's how I survived, 'cause I like to talk, as you can probably tell already, and that was my way of being able to communicate the happiness I was feeling without outing myself. And it was tough at first, but it became easier as time went on, and once that burden was gone, of being able to tell my parents that I was gay, and then being able to come out as a gay man and getting all of that baggage off of me, it was just like the weight of the world was lifted off me."* Nate's life has not been easy—his pension is tiny, his ex-wife is hostile, and his life partner lost a long, hard fight with cancer not long ago. But he prefers this situation to the secrets and lies (not to mention the health risks) of his job in the steel mills.

Nate is looking back at his life in the steel mill from an outsider's perspective. Being laid off forced him to find other work, and he chose work where he could be out. But even while in the mill, he was aware that his decision to remain closeted had a personal cost. The people I interviewed often discussed how their secret compromised their effectiveness at work, and their general quality of life. Jay attributes his alcoholism to the loneliness of the closet. Reflecting on his choices, he concludes: *"I'm sensitive. I'm real sensitive. I really want to be with somebody, but the only place I ever know of to go and meet somebody is a bar. But I've made up my mind, I'm going to get through this legal stuff and I'm going to get through this DUI, and then I'm going to meet someone. I'm going to live my life. And I've started telling people, 'You know what, I'm gay.' I don't lie about it anymore, but I have to be careful who I tell that to, where I tell it at, because around here there's a lot of prejudice."*

Zach, in contrast, was outed at work, and though this caused trouble at first, he has converted it into a personal victory. *"The first six years were pretty bad. I think every single vehicle I owned, and I switched a lot because of that, was keyed, dented, and I had one vehicle where lug nuts were removed, and I lost a tire. It was not fun. . . . Well [the outing] was funny, he was a good friend, but he seemed to have a fixation with if people were gay, he had a problem. And he was looking for fun online, and he met a girl I went to high school with in Lowell. . . . And her only good picture, is a picture of me and her when we went to a friend's wedding. And she's like 'well I've only got this one picture, it's me and a gay friend, and we're at this wedding.' So she emails it to him, and he says like 'that's [Zach]!' So that was his realization, and it just went through the whole rumor thing. . . . I had some friends that didn't talk to me for a while, they just didn't know how to take it, and I just had a lot of people come up later that were just like, 'I didn't know what to say, you know, you've always been a cool guy, you didn't act like it, you never made me feel uncomfortable, things like that, and it was just a shock and I didn't know what to say.' And then they come back and they're like, 'we're cool now.' But some of the in-between where you don't know and you just think, man, I just lost a whole bunch of good friends, for this?*

"You know . . . pretty much everyone's been cool, and even the ones that aren't, I've said 'hey, it's Mr. Faggot to you, I don't care what your problem is, it's your problem.' And a lot of the really strange ones always think that just because I'm gay and they're a man that I'm interested. I'm like no, no, it doesn't work that way. I'll just tell you flat out, right now, there's no interest, OK? We're good. I've even joked with a couple people when I'm changing, cause I've had the same locker for thirteen years, so everybody knows where my locker is. And I've had stuff drawn on there before, y'know like a big penis, and fag, stuff like that, but that all stopped. But I've actually joked with people, you know I'll get changed and I'll close my locker and I'm leaving and somebody else will be

changing and I'll be like, 'hey you better watch out there's a gay guy over there by that locker' and they just start laughing because they know it's me and I'm just making fun of it. I'm open and joke about it and it doesn't bother me any.

"It's your sense of humor that'll make or break ya. 'Cause if you can't joke, well it's just like with anything. If you show that it's bothering you people'll jump on it, and it doesn't matter what it is. You know if you're a woman and you're showing that that bothers you, or if you're gay or if you're black, anything, any little thing, it's just like grade school, you show any little weakness on something that bothers you, people will just pick up on that and y'know, drill you into the ground 'cause they know it bothers you. So that's what I did kind of early on, just kind of owned it, made it mine, joked about it, cause normally it's their problem with you and I just kind of turned it around so it's like no, it's my problem with you, you know. 'Cause I joke with people, I'm like 'you're cool even though you're straight, I don't hold that against ya.' And they're like 'whaat?' But that does it, you get somebody to laugh and then there's no more tension about it."

Zach has been able to create a sufficiently relaxed atmosphere in his circle of co-workers that they will laugh and joke about his sexuality too. He still feels lonely, however, reflecting that *"it would be nice to have somebody else to talk to. I mean, . . . I don't feel uncomfortable talking about anything at work, 'cause I check out some of the truck drivers and they all know my type too, so somebody new comes in, they're like 'you like him?' And they kind of get off on it, you know, cause you see it, I won't even be paying attention, I'll be eatin' or readin' or doing something and somebody'll come in and they know kind of what I like, and they're all kind of like <Zach indicates that they're pointing out this newcomer as a potential romantic interest for him> and they're all smiling and I look up and they're all looking at me and I'm like, 'what . . .* WHAT?' *And then I get the [point], and they want to see if I'm interested or not. And I'm like oh jeez, come on."*

Zach's story is inspiring, especially given all the tragedy and harassment experienced by the other steelworkers. But it's crucial to remember that he didn't choose visibility—it was thrust upon him. And he experienced six years of daily harassment and fear as its first consequence. His personal toughness and his sense of humor got him through and give his story a happy ending. And his good attitude is not rare—most of the steelworkers I interviewed are vibrant people, who love to tell a story and have clearly led interesting and satisfying lives. They emphasize their survival, rather than their difficulties. Yet in spite of their general optimism, most queer steelworkers keep the secret of their sexuality very carefully, noting that the people with whom they work make it abundantly clear that any variation from "normal" heterosexuality and "normal" gender roles will not be tolerated.

Managers share this sense of carefulness, though with some differences. As Lupe thinks back on her choices, she adds, *"So anyway, about being closeted at work. I don't really talk about it. If it was to come up, I think I'd handle it appropriately, but it just doesn't come up. It would be inappropriate to bring it up in most cases, so that's why it's not really talked about. I don't want to hit anyone over the head with being gay because it does make a lot of people uncomfortable, and if they're not ready to be confronted with it, then it's not really appropriate. I've never really been out about being straight either. When I was married, when I was dating, I was never really public. It could be a cowardly aspect of who I am at work, and other than the comments from other people at work, I think there's more protection at work for the bargaining unit people than there is for me, I really don't think that I would be fired for it, but I think that if there was someone who was uncomfortable with it, who was just fine not knowing, but then knew about it and saw me in a different light, perhaps that might cloud my next assignment. It could make them less cooperative on projects. So I think I'm a little more vulnerable as a management person than I would be as a union person. But, I would imagine other advantages too. I don't have any locker room issues."* Lupe feels some guilt about her choices, but also feels that they are justified by her circumstances, and by what she has seen happen to other workers.

Even when someone like Zach finds acceptance, it comes only after a long battle and at great personal cost, as the stories that opened this chapter testify. Other people choose to remain completely hidden, or to tell a few, carefully chosen friends. Lupe, who has worked in a mill for over twenty-five years, consciously decided to tell someone because *"we always had a good rapport. I felt that I could read that he would be OK. We have a lot in common. We worked a lot together, we still work together. After a while, you feel alone if nobody knows, so it was good to have somebody that knew."* She chose her allies carefully, and after years of caution, but for Lupe, there have been no repercussions, other than a sense of having an ally at last.

Finally, typical of many closeted steelworkers is Phil, who longs to come out at work, but doesn't want *"to be made an example of. To be standing there alone."* He is a young man who still has many years of work before retirement. He says he's *"tired of hearing fag this, and gay that"* and that, now, whenever he hears his co-workers engage in antigay banter, *"it makes the hair on my neck rise up."* He would love to be able to share news about his partner, to explain that all gay people do not correspond to stereotyped ideas, and to defend the other gay people he realizes must be hiding just as he is. His partner is a drag queen who performs frequently at the local gay bars, and it's a pleasure to see them together after her shows. They sit at the bar, she in full regalia next to Phil, big, with dirty fingernails, a baseball hat, and a beard, talking, laughing, enjoying each other's company.

It's a sight that makes me believe in the power of love, the power of change. Phil tells me that when he does come out, I can call him Dr. Martin Luther Queen. But for now, he is still scared and waiting until his mill feels like a safer, less hostile place.

CHAPTER FOUR

Female Masculinity in the Steel Mill

Everyone I spoke to who had experience in the integrated mills that produce basic steel agrees that mill work is "a man's world." But most also believe that certain women are completely capable of thriving there, and that plenty of men don't have what it takes. Toughness, humor, and an inclination toward teamwork seem to be what's required, and when circumstances or temperament cause these traits to occur in a women, she can do very well in this "man's world." Undine comments, nonchalantly, *"People make assumptions about women in there. It's a steel mill, not some nicey-nicey office job. We wear what we can get the job done in. And I'm always dirty."*

During World War II, many women entered heavy industry because of increased demand and a decreased workforce. With Rosie the Riveter as their representative, these women worked in shipyards, automotive plants, munitions factories, and practically every branch of heavy industry except the production of basic steel. Even with workers in such short supply that the prevailing patterns of gendered labor were relaxed, steel mills remained almost exclusively male domains (Olson 95). Legend had it that if a woman entered a steel mill, even for the sole purpose of delivering a forgotten lunch pail to her husband, the steel's composition would be undermined.

A 1974 consent decree, by which five major steel conglomerates agreed to increase female and minority presence in the mills in order to avoid being legally compelled to do so, is what introduced women into the steel manufacturing process. As Ruth Needleman demonstrates, the decree resulted from years of struggle by African American steelworkers within the union to curb racist practices in hiring and especially in promotion. "With more than four hundred discrimination cases pending before the Equal Employment Opportunity Commission, the USWA" agreed to the deal (205). U.S. Steel Gary Works had the highest proportion of female steelworkers, peaking at 12 percent in 1982 (Fonow 7). However, when the American steel industry collapsed during the recession of the early 1980s, women, the last to be hired, were disproportionately the first to be fired. Though women and African Americans fought to keep their jobs, they and the unions faced charges of reverse discrimination (Needleman 212). Those mills that still operate, albeit with a reduced labor force, again employ almost no women, and there is no movement afoot to change this pattern.

Thus, with the exception of the years between 1974 and 1984, the steel mills have been an almost exclusively male preserve, ubiquitously described as "a man's world." Jay summarizes his almost twenty years in the steel mill with this comment: *"The steel mill is a hard place to work, it's a harsh, harsh environment. Everyone expects you to be macho. You're supposed to be like a rough biker. You're not supposed to show your emotions, you're not supposed to cry. Anyone who's anybody drinks as far as the steel mill is concerned."* The women I interviewed share this view to an extent. They agree that the work is physically challenging and dangerous. As Erin states, *"You can't be a sissy about the weather out there,"* and Harriet notes that *"I had to be aware of myself constantly. . . . You didn't let them see any weakness. If you are just as tough as them, they leave you alone."* But these women are describing their work environment, not complaining. Their tone is one of satisfaction and survival. They're proud of their competence, telling stories of being put on labor crews and outlasting all the men, and of shoveling slag for eight- and even twelve-hour stretches. The women I interviewed fit their jobs well— manual labor, macho culture, and workplace camaraderie were things they enjoyed. These women are masculine, not to compete with or imitate men, but just because that's who they are—it works well for them.

Gender can be seen as a continuum, in which some people are exclusively masculine and others exclusively feminine, but most people fall somewhere in between. Because of job specifications, female steelworkers have short hair and fingernails and don't wear makeup at work. Given the dirt, heat, and physical labor, these and other markers of femininity would be impractical to the point of absurdity. Yet when I describe the steelworkers as masculine, I don't mean that they're not feminine. Like most women raised in our culture, they identified as women with pride and satisfaction. Traits like toughness, independence, and strength are stereotypically considered masculine, yet women who possess them aren't copying men, seeking to be men, or valuing men over women. And when I use the term "masculinity" to describe their self-presentation, I'm referring to this set of physical characteristics and behaviors, which—at least among steelworkers—is just as common in women as it is in men.

Judith Halberstam's assertion that "female-born people have been making convincing and powerful assaults on the coherence of male masculinity for years" (*Female Masculinity* 15) would meet with no argument from the steelworkers I interviewed. Erin joked, *"When I first went into the mill, I thought all the women were dykes because they all had hard hats on. They just all looked really tough."* Fern remembers being introduced to a work team with the warning, *"These two ladies, they look like dudes, but they're females, they're electricians."* Harriet reported responding to several situations by *"acting like one of the guys,"* adding that the women who made it in the mill *"had to physically work harder than most men. They were pushed, and only the tough ones survived."* All these women presented themselves with a masculine, butch style, both in appearance and mannerisms. Though several were quite short (5 feet tall or so) I tended to forget this fact when talking to them. They spoke with authority, took up generous amounts of space, and had a butch swagger, cockiness, and humor about them.

These masculine characteristics are common in female steelworkers, regardless of sexuality. According to Ben, *"Typically most men that are in the mill think that most women that are out on the production floor are lesbians, and most of them are not. Because they're in a man's job, so they think they're just lesbians."* Clearly, not all female steelworkers are lesbians, and not all lesbian steelworkers are masculine. As with all the steelworkers I interviewed, the lesbian ones are constantly negotiating the contradictions imposed on them by their cultures. To "fit in" at work, they need to be masculine, talk about sex in ways that objectify women, and endure severe and hazardous working conditions without whining. It's hard to believe that this is easier for them than it is for the gay male steelworkers I interviewed, since gay women told stories of harassment, assault, and even rape, yet they love their jobs and find satisfaction in their ability to fit in there. This "fit" is not mere perversity—it needs to be understood in context. For butch women with minimal education, any job they get is likely to be rough—the work world does not welcome butches warmly, especially in more menial jobs. Further, violence and danger are part of everyday life for many urban poor or working-class Americans. None of this means that lesbian steelworkers are not shocked or harmed by hostile work environments, yet it does help explain why working conditions that seem less than inviting can offer freedom and possibility to the women who occupy them.

Isabel reiterates: *"Steelworkers got to be big, they got to be tough, they got to be strong. The work they do is not for what you would consider a sissy or anything like that."* As with any job, or any other social structure, mill work expresses a series of promises to its participants: if you can behave within the approved parameters, you will gain acceptance. In basic steel mills, those parameters include masculine behavior—talking about sex, responding aggressively to teasing, enduring hardship without complaint, drinking. Lesbian steelworkers who exhibit these traits struggle with the

Electrician, #3 AC Station, Indiana Harbor Works, East Chicago.
Courtesy of the Calumet Regional Archives.

contradictions they imply. Fitting into a man's world makes them vulnerable to rape and sexual harassment, acting like "one of the boys" devalues women and therefore themselves, and being expected to brag about sex with women turns their sexuality into the object of voyeuristic display. Though my narrators are usually comfortable in their jobs and work settings, finding a degree of acceptance there that would be impossible for them in more traditionally feminine workplaces, these contradictions remain an ongoing part of how they live and work.

For these gay women, a tradition of female masculinity tied not to copying men but rather to doing a good job, being who you are, and establishing workplace rapport exists in the mills—but not without repercussions, unfortunately, since all of these women are punished somehow for their assumption of masculinity. In spite of these costs, they manifest palpable pleasure, satisfaction, and pride in their work. As one labor historian notes, "For pioneer blue-collar women a key to success was to like the work the way a man does, do it the way a man does, and not let any background limitations or sex-related problems get in the way" (Walshok 197). Some might argue that this lets men set the terms, with women imitating them, but the women I interviewed find in mill work an expression of themselves—satisfaction with a job well done—unrelated to men. In steel mills, then, "masculinity does not belong to men, has not been produced only by men, and does not properly express male heterosexuality" (Halberstam, *Female Masculinity*, 241). What this means for men is complicated, a question considered in the next chapter. But Gail summarizes the women's attitude: *"The mill's been a fascinating place. It's been very good to me. I can't complain. I don't think any of the women can complain."*

Masculine appearance and behavior have historically been among the ways lesbians identify, and are identified. Elizabeth Lapovsky Kennedy and Madeline D. Davis, in their detailed study of the lesbian community in Buffalo, conclude that attraction to women as romantic and sexual partners came to define the lesbian only secondarily; adopting the male gender role came first, and was more salient. They draw from the work of George Chauncey, who detects a shift in the early twentieth century from defining homosexuality via gender inversion to defining it by object choice. For working-class lesbians, this emphasis meant that butches faced "severe stress and pressure created by the attempt to publically validate lesbian life and to claim more space for lesbians" (Kennedy and Davis 321). Jealousy and violence were one result of this stress, but another was the choice of working-class, manual labor jobs. Precisely because these jobs were dirty, dangerous, and often poorly paid, butch lesbians (turned down for anything visible or prestigious) could get them. Further, they could continue to wear uniforms, pants, and short hair at work. That these women didn't have to "straighten up" in order to hold jobs contributed to their coherent sense of lesbianism as an identity, and thus to the "consciousness of kind" prerequisite to gay liberation. Of my twenty lesbian narrators, most were extremely masculine, and I can't imagine them passing for straight at work, or anywhere else for that matter. The remaining few were also pretty tough, but more tentative. At least their shoulders weren't thrown back in that classic butch confrontational/come-hither persona. They all wore boots.

Though not all women in uniform are lesbians, they all benefit to some extent from the masculinity attributed to lesbians. *Hard-Hatted Women* anthologizes, as its subtitle explains, women's "Stories of Struggles and Success in the Trades" in the form of first-person narratives. The book's one steelworker lyrically describes her work experiences, and how it feels to be "part of something BIG" (Martin 62). She "enjoyed so much the banter, the camaraderie, the oneness of mill life" (62). Though she reveals nothing about her sexuality, like my narrators, she sounds tough, independent, and masculine, which is why lesbians seem like such a natural fit for these jobs. Fern remembers asking what heavy equipment operators do when deciding whether to apply for their training program. Her response to the reply was *"Oh toys, cool. Dirt, toys, OK!"* and she loves the work. Her face lights up and the whole room comes alive when she describes her job. As Embrick, Walther, and Wickens observe, in their research on working-class masculinity, "If lesbians were to gain employment in a hyper-masculine industry, the men who worked with them would feel more comfortable with them than they would with gay men" (763). This does not mean that the blue-collar work situation for lesbians is rosy. Embrick, Walther, and Wickens go on to demonstrate that all but straight white males are anathema to working-class workplaces, even those in which workers and management verbally appear very progressive. Thus, to say that the situation is better for lesbians is not to say that it is good.

Several lesbian steelworkers describe a struggle for acceptance in which they are effectively demonstrating masculinity in order to keep their jobs. Athena sets the stage: *"It's very hard being a woman in the mill. You have to understand the dynamics of the mill. You have the good ol' boys' club. It's a man's world. [The assumption is that] you're invading the man's world, you're taking a job from my son, or my cousin, or my brother, or the guy down the street. Women shouldn't be here. Because women are here, we can't have our* Playboy *magazines, and watch our porno movies when we're on break. And that's all women's fault—that's our fault. They have to watch their language. I mean, they make up excuses. You have some people that are just fine with women being there, and you still do have some that are not."* In this setting, women's survival depends on their acting masculine.

Like most women in the mills, Janis was hired as a laborer, in her case in a slabber, and the work she did was physical, and very demanding. *"I was young and strong then, way stronger than I am now. The bricks came in in 100-pound blocks. We had to open up these bundles, and they'd be perforated into four twenty-five-pound units. I'd hit the block <acts out a chipping motion> with my hand to separate it, then pass the twenty-five-pound block to the next person on my labor gang. We had to do this very fast. Sometimes we'd have to replace the bricks inside the pits. They'd still be hot, 'cause they kept the heat inside 'em for a long time. When we went down in there, we'd have to wear thermal shirts under our long-sleeved shirts, 'cause otherwise, if someone's arm brushed the side, it'd burn the skin right off. So we were working in this hot, enclosed space wearing layers of clothes, doing back-breaking work. It was hard enough being a woman in that job.*

"So I wanted to get out of there, and I took some classes, and passed all the tests to train as electrical. And I had accumulated enough seniority and had a

good work record. They didn't want to give me the promotion, and they kept trying not to, but ultimately they had no choice.

"The day before I was scheduled to begin my apprentice training there, they tried to block me. On top of each soaking pit there was pea gravel, to protect it? That day they told me to replace the pea gravel. It came in 100-pound bags. I asked, 'Can I use a wheelbarrow?' and they said OK. So I opened the bag, poured some in the wheelbarrow, rolled it over to the first pit, and started hauling it up there. They thought they could get rid of me, but I found a way." Like many successful female steelworkers, Janis faced hardships, but rather than complain, or quit, she worked around them, thereby proving herself tough enough for the job.

Fern notes that there are very few women in the construction trades, and even fewer are heavy equipment operators. Only the most masculine women (and men) survive. *"In our local of operating engineers, we cover part of Iowa, and northeast Illinois, and Indiana to the Ohio border, we're maybe 23,000 members strong, across three states. Females, operators alone, make up about 150 females, and that might be shooting a little high. Of all the construction trades altogether, women make up about 1 percent. And that might be a little ambitious."* When I asked why female operators are so rare, she replied, *"I think it comes down more to the fact, you've got to have a tougher outer skin. When your foreman gets in your face and starts screaming and yelling and telling everyone they're stupid, dumb, idiot, 'What the heck, I told you to do this, I don't understand the problem, can you guys not manage to do this?' and starts throwing stuff and pitching a fit, y'know, I don't mean to sound sexist, and don't take this the wrong way, a lot of women can't take it. I've been on jobs where there is other females, not operators, but they're laborers, or steelworkers, and the foreman will come up and lay into them and you just start watching 'em. I'll walk up and go 'whatever you do, don't cry.' I'm not trying to be mean, and I'm not trying to be insensitive, but if you can't take, as they say, a true asschewing, this isn't the field for you. A lot of women I know, I don't think they can cut it."* Fern believes the ability to take *"a true ass-chewing"* without crying is rare in women. Most lesbians and gender-nonconforming women have had ample exposure to public attacks and humiliation, especially in inhospitable working-class environments, which makes them well equipped for this type of work setting. And lesbians are motivated to get and keep these jobs, since "lesbians have greater family-based incentives than do straight women to aim for full-time, better-paid jobs, even if they violate some gender norms in the process" (Badgett and King 78). Thus, cultural and economic factors contribute to the link between female masculinity and lesbians in the steel mills.

Mary Lindenstein Walshok has done a pioneering study of blue-collar women in which she concludes that most women who end up in masculine, nontraditional jobs first "broke pattern" as teens (90). The women she studied did this in various ways and for different reasons, but none were traditionally "girlie" (89). For 10 percent of her sample, this pattern-breaking includes lesbian identification, which Walshok argues is not so much because lesbians tend to be masculine as because lesbians foresee a lifelong need to be self-supporting and many traditionally feminine jobs don't enable financial independence. In addition, lesbians, by the time of employment, have sufficient "practice living as an outsider" (109) to insulate them somewhat from the harassment all women in these nontraditional jobs will inevitably face. As Athena says, *"The women that are in the mills don't think they can be senior operators or techs. You have a few that do. Lesbians are more likely to think they can do these jobs. 'Cause it is easier for a lesbian, 'cause yes, we need the money, and we have a different attitude. We know what we're getting into. We've been discriminated before. We've been discriminated as women, we've been discriminated as gay."*

Lesbian steelworkers expect such harassment as part of their work culture. They almost look for it and, if they respond appropriately, expect to succeed in their jobs. Olshana hired in as an apprentice motor inspector, which is a skilled trade, and a highly coveted job where women have not made significant inroads. She tells this story: *"The first day I got there to work I had to lubricate motors on a roll line, and I remember I had to walk on this really dangerous catwalk between the rollers to lubricate and it was scary, it was dangerous, and I was wondering if it was an attempt to scare me away. I can't say that it was, but at the time I thought maybe it was. I didn't know where to lock the machine out or anything like that, I felt really vulnerable, and I did it. I think it just showed, which I did, that if you were willing to put up with some dangerous conditions and didn't start to cry, or didn't complain and just do it, a lot of the resistance that guys had to a woman being around would dissolve if they saw that you were willing to throw yourself in. That was my experience. I didn't get too much, like any sort of lethal hostility."* Neither the danger nor the testing surprised or intimidated her, and she credits this reaction with communicating her adequacy to her male colleagues.

Nonwhite women, both gay and straight, have even more experience with harassment and systematic oppression. Back when blacks first entered the mills during World War II, there was a clear division of labor along racial lines. According to Erin, this persisted until the 1974 consent decree, which is *"when they stopped their racist policies of putting all the black people in the coke ovens. Which is where you see really high levels of cancer.*" Though all black workers were restricted to the most dangerous jobs with the least opportunity for advancement, "it was necessary to masculinize black women by attributing to them characteristics such as strong and husky" (Fonow 30). Though masculinization functions in this context as a tool to divide women, it and the attendant public censure can also open up a space that masculine women can step into. Thus, it's less relevant that lesbian steelworkers tend to be masculine than that lesbians have experience being hassled and have learned to handle that without demonstrating weakness.

Janis faced harassment for being female, and for being a communist. Then, people found out she was gay. She says most of the workers, once they got to know her, didn't cause much trouble—that mostly came from the higher-ups. "*But there was this big Lithuanian guy. He had heard I had a girlfriend and he jumped me. We would have to take this bus from the parking lot to where we were working. You would have to allow about an extra half hour before your shift for that transportation. But he came up and jumped me when we were waiting for the bus. But I knew some Judo and I flipped him over, right in front of the bus. And right in front of the other guys. But then he jumped me again, and I had this pipe with me, and I whipped it around that quick and had his hat off. I said, 'That could have been your head.'*" She describes one further incident with this guy, but stresses that he, and the other men watching, learned from her aggressive, direct responses that she was there to work and could defend herself.

When Gail began her career as a steelworker at a Bethlehem coal mine near Philadelphia, she was one of seven women hired in 1975 in response to the consent decree. They were not welcome. These women were directed into the "*cage*" (i.e., elevator) and gradually lowered into a mine that descended 3,000 feet. "*I found out that some of the guys around there ran to the top of the area where the cage was and took bets on how many women were going to scream to get out, and how far down they'd go before they started screaming. Actually, none of us screamed to get out. We all went down. And none of us quit.*" Gail describes the work she did in great detail, and with evident pride and satisfaction. She didn't persist in this nontraditional job because of money or convenience, but because of a fit between her tough, get-the-job-done temperament and the tasks she faced in mill and mine.

Often women in the mills were worked harder than men, even given the more dangerous assignments, but rather than quitting, they generally out-toughed the men who challenged them. Kate fits this pattern, noting that she's never had problems from men at work, "*especially once I got in and*

Open-hearth furnace, Inland Steel, East Chicago, mid-1970s.
Courtesy of the Calumet Regional Archives.

started working, the guys would rather work with me than some of the other guys, because I'm a workhorse. If she's there, you know she's there to work. I'm not going to turn around and she's going to be gone. Or she's not going to be saying, I can't do that." I assume there were many women who didn't remain in the mills for long, who found the physical work and/or the shaming too much to take. By seeking out lesbian narrators, one could argue that I'm selecting for female masculinity, by concentrating on those who survived. However, Kay Deaux and Joseph C. Ullman's 1983 study, *Women of Steel*, is based on interviews with 104 female steelworkers, none of whom identifies as a lesbian in the book, and they report minimal sexual harassment. Some women describe problems with men early in their employment, but they dealt with it effectively themselves. One tells a story of a co-worker who "came up and asked if I needed any money. Then he put a brand new $100 bill in my hand. I threw it right back. 'It's not enough money and you're not enough man,' I told him. He's never bothered me since" (134).

Deaux and Ullman conclude that female steelworkers have fewer problems than one might expect because "women in the blue-collar environment have more relative power than women in many occupations, and also have more direct ways to cope with initial advances that male workers might make" (134). This sense that all female steelworkers exercise power, control, and confidence at work, thereby breaking the confines of traditional gender in ways that could be called queer, is echoed by a video documentary produced in 1985, also titled *Women of Steel*. It features a boilermaker named Sherry Ortallono, who says the hardest thing for her was "to learn how to burn. At times you had to have a very steady hand. It took me a little time to get that confidence in burning. I have two guys from work to thank for that." She reflects that "a girl is raised to smile and be nice, but I found that the more I fought back with them, the more they respected me." Though the film doesn't identify Ortallono as straight, our cultural assumption that you are straight unless identified otherwise implies that she is. Yet she made it in a very tough apprenticeship by working with her colleagues, thriving in that setting, and fighting back when required. The masculine behaviors I've been describing are not, then, limited to lesbians. Though identifying female steelworkers as masculine doesn't, of course, mean they're all lesbians, it does mean that lesbians can easily slide into these jobs, experiencing a comfortable fit, rather than the awkward adjustment required of many lesbians in "women's jobs."

A good example of this fit is provided by Gail, who reports working to ensure that the other workers knew and respected her. *"There were still a few millwrights I worked with that I had to convince I was OK. One of them was a little guy they called Weasel. He was short and very thin and very wiry and very hyperactive. And even though he was about sixty years old he was still very hyperactive, and a very good millwright. And he did not want to work with me. They sent me to him. Well, he dropped a gear casing, that weighed about seventy pounds, on my thumb, and the guy that we were working with said he thought he did it on purpose. And it just split my thumb and fractured the bone, and the bone actually splintered and went off in two different directions. And I went into their dispensary, and they took X-rays, and they were going to put me off work and put it in a cast, and I said, 'Oh no you're not, you're going to put a splint on it and send me back to work.' When I went back to work, everybody was shocked that I was back. They thought that for sure I'd be on workman's comp and I said, 'Nah, it's only a thumb.' I went directly to the tool room, got a length of rope, and I almost hung that guy. I knew where we were working and I went on a catwalk above him and I had just a real simple noose made, and I dropped it around him, and I gave it a yank and wrapped it around, and he was on his toes screaming. I can't remember exactly what I said to him, because I used a lot of colorful language, and I said, 'If you ever hurt me again, I won't stop. I'll take this rope up even higher.' After that, even though I was assigned to work with him, we worked together, but we didn't as-sociate at all.*" Since filing a complaint would have been less effective, Gail assumed the authority for her own protection, thereby gaining acceptance from the culture in which she worked. And, as she tells it, Gail and Weasel subsequently got to be, if not friends, at least amiable co-workers. Follow-ing an episode where she helped out by cleaning up his tools, she notes with satisfaction, *"After that, he asked to work with me."*

Many of my lesbian narrators have stories like this one—stories about es-tablishing themselves by giving as good as they got, or better. Harriet quips, *"You know how they say 'Suck my dick'? I just pulled my shorts down and said, 'Suck my clit.'"* Walshok's research confirms what these steelworkers' sto-ries suggest. She believes that blue-collar women may have an advantage in highly masculine work settings like the mills, since slaps and other direct approaches to harassment stop it more effectively than formal remedies do, and physical, aggressive behavior is part of blue-collar culture (239). As Walshok puts it, "In order to cut it, you have to go with the norms of the dominant group" because they provide a structure for interaction, without which culture tends to play out its gender dominance script (232). By this model, my narrators' masculine demeanor derailed their co-workers strat-egy of trying to eliminate them through harassment and intimidation. Kate says that her partner sometimes objects to her constant profanity, saying *"You're not among the boys now."* In the mill, she explains, *"we use 'fuck' as an all-purpose word,"* which Kate grew up with, since both of her parents were steelworkers, so their home language was *"pretty raw."* Foul language is one way that Kate feels included and comfortable in the masculine work culture.

A shared attraction to women provides another means by which lesbian steelworkers can foster community in the masculine environment of the mills. Fern tells many stories that reflect this type of interaction, noting that she wasn't hassled for being gay. *"If anything,* she says of her male co-workers, *"they embraced it."* Summarizing the reactions she has gotten to being out at work, she said, *"I've really had no problems. I've had nothing but, 'Cool, thumbs up, that's awesome.' I think the biggest complaint they've had with me about being gay is I take their air fresheners. You know I'll get in the scrapers [backhoes], and they'll have these air fresheners, those ones with naked women, and I'll think, 'Oooh, that's kind of a cute one,' and I'll take it. They'll get back in the machine, and they're like, 'Hey my air freshener's gone.' And the first thing they do is they come straight to me 'cause, one, I'm the only female, and, two, they know I'm gay. They say, 'Can I have my air freshener* back?' 'No, I like it.' So then they get a good laugh and chuckle. They feel they can be themselves. They can laugh and joke about pretty much anything and they know I'm not going to get offended. At first, when I get onto a job that I've never worked with the guys, they are kind of edgy, 'cause they don't know, but when they do find out, it's just like, 'hey, cool beans.'" Fern here inserts herself into, rather than challenges, the male sexual economy of the workplace. She brings sex with women into the mill as a "price of admission" to the work culture.

Nate worked with very few women, but he notes that "some of the ladies that we had there were rough and tumble. They had to be. And some of them were almost as inappropriate as some of the men, y'know, as far as sexualizing the environment." His comments demonstrate that, Fern's acceptance aside, lesbian steelworkers may sometimes have been more comfortable with their own masculine behavior than their male co-workers were.

In Fern's experience, mill workers save their homophobia for men, who don't incorporate well into their sexual fantasies and consequently get shunned. She speculates that "most men, when you think of what their sexual fantasies are, what are they? Usually a guy and a girl, or a girl and a girl, right? So, to work with a gay woman is not a threat to them. They find it more interesting and exciting. The possibilities, maybe. Not necessarily all guys, but y'know. Men's sexual fantasies are girl and girl, well you get a lesbian on the job, well, guess what? There's half of it right there, you know. And they feel they can be more themselves. They can look at the women go by, they can make their comments, and I'm going to be able to pretty much relate to it, y'know. They can talk about their problems with their wife being bitchy or moody or irritable, or wanting this or that, and most gay women can relate to that, 'cause at some point we deal with women all the time too. So, y'know. But gimme a gay guy, and there are not too many people have fantasies about two guys together except gay guys. And I am sure that makes a lot of men very uncomfortable because it's not a fantasy they'd have. I'm personally sure that's where the difference is." What makes Fern's interactions so trouble-free is not just that she likes girls, but also that she is comfortable discussing it, even if this makes her own sexuality the voyeuristic object of a male gaze.

Yesenia observes that she is somewhat immune to harassment, partly because she has been around for a while and is thus unconcerned about other people's opinions of her, and partly because she is willing to treat harassment as a game, and retaliate rather than feel victimized. "For me it's pretty easy 'cause I've been out forever, so it's like 'what're you gonna say to me that I haven't already heard?' But most people are pretty cool. Got a lot *of 'em, older workforce that work with me . . . and so one day, a co-worker of mine and I, he's a guy, a real southern boy, he knew about me because I think something happened one day and someone brought me lunch and he's like, 'is that your girlfriend?' and I go, 'yes it is.' And he was like, "Ohhh, alright, well if you got any other ones bring 'em over,' and he's like 'she's got a big chest,' and I was like, 'Oh you're an ass," and I used to shoot the shit with him and I used to call him a hillbilly guy all the time and stuff."* Since the mills are defined as male space, sex is defined as intercourse with women. This makes lesbians (at least those willing to discuss their "conquests") more acceptable than gay men, and even more easy to integrate into conversations than straight women would be.

Given that mill workers, like many other blue-collar workers, spend so much time together shoveling, waiting, and doing mindless tasks as a group, conversation is crucial to mitigate the boredom. This situation means that the division between work life and home life erodes, since everything ultimately becomes grist for the conversational mill. It also means that lesbians who are willing to be casual and confident about their social and sexual behavior add entertainment, and even an erotic thrill, to the workday. Undine explains, *"We joke around at work. We smack each other. I work with the crane operators a lot 'cause I got to get them to move things around for me. This one guy, I told him, 'I always got to be on top,' and now they tease me about that. There's definitely a joking atmosphere."* She adds, *"I like my job."*

The female steelworkers I interviewed confirm Walshok's observation that working-class women are part of an aggressive culture where sexual banter passes time and physical contact is not anathema. These women often used masculine personality traits to handle the situations they encountered effectively—aggressive behavior and physical contact served them well. Gail relates how she dealt with harassment, once by rotating a swivel chair to *"whack him in the nuts"* and once in a more public setting. *"There was a guy they named Spider. We'd be up in what we call the pulpit—it's a big room inside the mill, where we keep all of our equipment—our control room. This one was very large because we had a lot of equipment, and plus, there was like four, five people working there at the time. And he'd always, if I said something smart to him, because he'd usually say something smart to me and I'd say something smart back, he'd grab his crotch and he says, 'Here.' And he did that to me one day, and I smiled at him and I walked over, and he thought I was going to say something to him, and I came up with my hand right into his crotch and I grabbed his crotch and I squeezed as hard as I could, and I drug him about twenty feet down through the pulpit, him on his tiptoes yelling and screaming all the way. And I said, 'You're going to learn a lesson, buddy.' Any time any guy transferred in after that, he'd tell them, 'Don't mess with her—here's what she did to me.' After that, he made sure I never had that problem. He'd tell all the guys."* To conclude her stories about harassment, Gail notes, *"I really didn't have any problems. I imagine straight girls have more problems."*

Olshana also claims that she faced no serious problems or harassment at work. *"There were a few sort-of like hard core experiences. Ordinary sort of backwards guys that if you just reacted in an appropriate way, they wouldn't bother you again. If you showed you weren't going to—if you talk back to them and show that you won't take verbal abuse, and make a point of giving it back in the same way, they wouldn't mess with you anymore. I never got physically pushed or shoved or anything like that. One guy one time touched my ass. We were walking together, going to a job—he just reached down and touched my ass and I just <elbows back>, it was just my instinct, I didn't even think about it, I elbowed him. It wasn't even a conscious thought. He touched me and I just really elbowed him, and he never did anything like that again. I tried to fit in. I didn't complain. I tried to learn."* Like Gail, she emphasizes her resolution of the incident—her ability to control the situation—rather than on the climate that allowed it to occur. A slight shift in emphasis could have made the same stories accounts of constant vigilance, rather than of nonchalant capability.

Further, Gail implies that direct contact between straight women and male *"nuts"* might cause more problems than it prevents. Do straight women respond with the boldness and physicality that these lesbians report and, if so, with what results? Remember that neither Harriet, who quipped *"suck my clit,"* nor Gail, who did this grab-and-twist-act, are out at work. But does a presumed lesbianism somehow make them safe, and thus able to pull it off? I would argue that this confidence comes from the work, not from sexuality. When any woman makes it in this masculine job, she finds satisfaction and confidence within herself, which earns her respect. The workers portrayed in *Women of Steel* "were satisfied with their job, often finding it a source of challenge and a marked improvement over other jobs that they had held. . . . Although laboratory research often finds women underestimating their performance relative to men, these steel women regarded themselves on a par with men on most dimensions that we assessed" (Deaux and Ullman 144). In both appearance and mannerisms, then, all female steelworkers might be thought of as honorary lesbians.

In their study of gay and lesbian graduates of the Harvard Business School, Annette Friskopp and Sharon Silverstein identify a "lesbian advantage." One subject observes: "People at work view me as appropriately aggressive and dedicated to my work. Men don't misread my attempts to build relationships as having sexual connotations" (372). Another notes that "the role and style freedom that comes with lesbianism puts me head and shoulders over most heterosexual women" (373). Though these lesbian MBAs don't describe the sexual banter and disclosure reported by mill workers, they do benefit from stereotypes of lesbians as temperamentally masculine and as filling a masculine role in the sexual economy of the workplace. Harriet, one of my narrators who stayed pretty well closeted in the mills, relates that when she transferred to a new section, members of her new crew removed the pornography that had been hanging on the walls (though only after she got an eyeful on her initial tour). During her first days with this crew, *"they pointed out that there was a lesbian working there who didn't mind the pictures. She even told them what she did with her girlfriend. She told them stories about her dildo, and they had no problem with that."* These accounts made Harriet anxious, since she didn't know how to interpret them: was this an invitation to disclose her identity and advance notice that it wouldn't be a problem? She experienced the stories more as a warning; she had already been raped by co-workers once, when she worked at a previous job, and so she knows that no amount of cockiness will keep her safe. Throughout the steelworkers' stories, pornography serves to reinforce heterosexual male power; even the most accepted steelworkers, such as Olshana, who had *"fun going to strip clubs with the guys after work,"* report seeing pornography and worrying about it.

Accounts of mill life describe pornography as pervasive. Deborah Rudacille's detailed history of the Sparrows Point mill near Baltimore explains how constant exposure to hard-core pornography affected the women hired after the consent decree (1974). "There was pornography everywhere, absolutely everywhere," Mary Ellen Beechner said. "I remember walking into one shop where I was going to do some lead sampling to make sure people weren't being overexposed, and they had pictures from *Hustler* magazine, I mean really hard-core stuff, wallpapering the walls. I put my hand on the table and it was all over the tables, under plastic and all. I felt so uncomfortable" (167–68). Similarly, Harriet describes areas of the mill covered *"in pictures of naked women, and some of them were drawn on with the white pencils we use to mark the sheets. Crass stuff—just really nasty. They would be giving blow jobs and worse. All I said was, 'They must not keep you very busy up here.'"*

For these women, detachment feels like a better strategy than intervention. Even Fern, usually comfortable with sexual banter, reveals that *"I had*

a crew that was so very comfortable with me being gay and did not feel threat-
ened by me, they brought porns to work. They brought their portable DVDs *to*
watch. Course now, you know, there's a line you draw. I said if you guys want
to watch this, y'know. They said 'you're gay, and you're cool with it, right?' I
said, 'Wait a second, that's what you guys want to watch, at work? So be it,
I'm not going to be offended by it. But if anything goes down and you guys get
in trouble for having inappropriate material at work, I had nothing to do with
it.'" Without losing face as an unflappable "one of the guys," Fern resists
involvement with pornography at work. As Erin adds, *"it was hard enough*
to be female in the mill, and to sort of hold my own." Keeping a casual, masculine attitude about sex made this process easier, but even for butch lesbians,
"there's a line you draw."

The Pleasure of Butchness

M. V. Lee Badgett and Mary C. King, in "Lesbian and Gay Occupational
Strategies," come to some expected, and some fascinating, conclusions. For
example, they note that lesbians are more heavily concentrated in "craft/
operative jobs than heterosexual women" are (82). This concentration
might indicate that lesbians are more willing to trade gender conformity
for increased money and benefits, if their data didn't show that lesbians
in these jobs in fact earn *less* than the average wage. Badgett and King are
left wondering "why lesbians appear to be clustered in relatively poor paying and intolerant occupations" (82). Since their analysis is a traditional
economic one, they don't explore preferences motivated by temperament,
personality, or "fit." The women I interviewed do difficult jobs and struggle
financially. Their work involves regular layoffs, ill health, inconvenient
schedules, and dirt. But they love it, at least in part because it expresses the
masculinity that's a crucial part of who they are.

Successful mill workers, both male and female, are those who can "play
with the big boys." They are not easily intimidated, expect a fair amount of
harassment as part of the work culture, and respond to this environment
with humor and a willingness to participate. All the workers I met who
continued working in the mills past the first few months are masculine.
"Masculine" is one of those terms that resist definition except by recourse
to their opposite. To be masculine is to be whatever your time and place
defines as not feminine. Esther Newton defines butch identity as fluid, powerful, and derived from its contexts. "Being butch was the first identity that
had ever made sense out of my body's situation, the first rendition of gender

that ever rang true, the first look I could ever pull together. Butches may have been laughable to straight people and an embarrassment to the uptown dykes, but in the bar life they were citizens, they were mensches, and they were hot" (*Margaret Meade Made Me Gay*, 207). According to Newton, the bars were working-class spaces where butch became a viable, meaningful identity because it communicated something about sexuality to an inhospitable world, and because it expressed something about sexuality to other queers through the act of being seen and desired. To summarize Judith Halberstam, female masculinity is not women borrowing clothes or behaviors from men, but women inhabiting the clothes or behaviors pervasively claimed by men. Inhabiting those clothes because they fit—they "make sense" out of the "body's situation."

For some gay women I interviewed, working in the steel mills provides an opportunity to give full expression to their masculinity, and get paid for it rather than punished. They parallel the butches described by Kennedy and Davis who fought to keep their masculine appearance though that appearance meant most jobs were not available to them. "They left the jobs that required skirts and sought jobs that would let them dress the way that they wanted. They worked in factories . . . that did not care what women wore to work" (86). When industries were forced to hire women, many of these butches got steady work for the first time (88). When I worked as a mechanic, my uniform, especially when dirty, frequently led people to think I was a man. I didn't mind—I liked it. Putting on the uniform, especially the steel-toed boots, shaped the way I walked, talked, and felt. I loved the feeling of competence that came with the higher salary of doing "man's work." Cars would come in "on the hook," and after I worked on them, the grateful owners came in and drove them away. My satisfaction at doing something so visibly helpful, and so out of the reach of the average person, was inextricably tied to the gender associated with the job. The amount of pure joy and satisfaction these lesbian steelworkers exude when describing their jobs demonstrates a similar fit between personality and occupation.

For example, Fern describes her work as a heavy equipment operator: *"The job itself is no harder than driving a car. It's the mental. That part means, you need to know what that machine can do, what its limitations are, how far you can take that machine. You've got to know how it operates. You've got to be able to know where everybody is at all times. You have to be able to carry a grade. Mind you, I'm five foot tall. Most standard end loaders their tires are eight feet tall. That's an average end loader. You climb up in that seat way up there, you can't see over the edge of that bucket. They tell you they want that to grade. You're going to have to put it to grade. You know how a level works? Watch for the bubble, when it gets in the middle you know you're level? That's what operators do. You literally have to have what they call bubble butt. You have to feel it—just the slightest pitch, you're going to be able to feel."* Rather than being an obstacle, her size is part of the process—something to work with to get a sense of mastery and accomplishment. If she were taller, she could see what she was working on, and *"making the grade"* would be easier. Instead of opting out of the job, however, she devises a system of using other parts of her body to provide the data she needs to accomplish her task. And describing this process makes her feel proud and happy.

The lesbian steelworkers took a visceral pleasure from doing these jobs—they describe individual projects with childish delight. Gail tells a story about removing the large bolts from polishers. *"We used some pneumatic tools to take the nuts off, but to get the bolts out, you actually have to stand on top, after you get the nut off, you rotate them around on top. And then some people get up there with sledgehammers—hammer 'em out. That was my job. They gave me the sledgehammer. I had a ball with it. You learn to do a lot of amazing things. It was fun. It was a job you actually woke up and enjoyed going to."*

Lakisha, who hasn't worked in the mill for ten years, remembers *"you had your uniform, and I had this safety inspector uniform, it was actually a fire retardant, like this ugly green color. I kept all that stuff. Gear is fun. And I had the steel-toed boots, probably a couple of pairs."* She doesn't need these garments in her current job, but they remind her of an exciting, adventurous time, one where her masculinity could be expressed through clothes and through work.

Finally, Harriet describes a special project she worked on. *"At Mittal, I was a laborer for a few months, and then they put me on a special project. A thirteen million buck project to produce the steel plates for the wind generators. You know, those turbines they're putting up in central Indiana? We were making product and we had a goal to get it done within the budget. Part way through, they found they could get them cheaper from China, and they did that for a while. But then that product didn't meet standards, which ours did. And we kept to the target. Yes, we got lots of pats on the back and 'good jobs' for that one."* All of my narrators, both gay men and gay women, had this pride in their jobs: a sense of competence derived from surviving and thriving in a tough work environment. These lesbians also had an added sense of having found, sometimes after long struggle, a home.

However, not all lesbians, and not even all butch lesbians, experienced this fit and its accompanying job satisfaction. Carmen is very butch: she is a tall, imposing woman with salt-and-pepper dreadlocks, an aggressive swagger to her walk, and a verbal reticence that gives the impression she is talking about herself and her feelings only under pressure. It's as though each word is an effort—she hardly opens her mouth when she *does* talk. Yet she is adamant that *"the steel mills are no place for women—our bodies are not equipped to do that work."* She took the job decades ago because she needed the money, and she kept it for that reason only. She says that every one of her supervisors hated her for being a woman and for being black. They tried to make her quit by giving her the hardest and most dirty jobs. She adds that *"when I was pregnant, they put me on a job shifting billets in an outdoor yard, and I lost my baby."* She was *"mad as hell"* but she still refused to quit, and continued to work in the mill until she was injured (burned over 60 percent of her body) and left with a full pension. Though she is as masculine as anyone I interviewed, she never felt the comfort or acceptance that many other women talk of, though she smiles to herself as she recalls that she did win out in the end.

Masculine women experience frequent harassment in daily life. Most poignantly, Isabel reports that *"I really keep to myself and look down because I don't want to be harassed and I don't want to see the weird looks or anything like that."* She's describing daily life in Northwest Indiana, where *"I live in my little bubble so I don't have to see it."* Given this context, mill work is a source of freedom. Important work done well, in a setting where female masculinity is an asset rather than a liability, makes new ways of doing gender and sex possible. Halberstam acknowledges that "as the complicated lives of some masculine women show, there are also ways for women to pioneer forms of masculinity that change the meaning of modern gender and sexual identity" (*Female Masculinity* 109).

Wanda dresses and presents herself in an overtly masculine way, and meets with a correspondingly high level of harassment, both in and especially out of the mill. To our interview, she wore a tie, a scrupulously neat button-down shirt, a sweater, and a paperboy cap, whose plaid pattern exactly picked up the teal blue of her sweater. Style is clearly important to her, and she's good at it—she seemed calm, confident, and at home in her skin. She reports that, though there have been rough patches, she has found more acceptance at the mill than she has at home, or in the community. *"But at the mill I feel like it's my family. Everyone knows. Some people I talk to, and then some I don't but they know. They don't really press the issue, because they know that it's violating my civil rights to be comin' in my face talking about that in the mill. When I first got hired, I remember HR . . . told me, she said, hey, if you have any problems, you contact labor relations. I'm sitting there, like, OK. And she said it again, and I say OK. I went to the interview just like this, except I had on dress slacks, and she let me know indirectly, that she knew, you are a lesbian, and something might come up, and do not be scared to tell some one. That was a company person. The union, like I said, has took me in their arms.*" Though Wanda has never filed a formal harassment complaint, she has approached the authorities when pushed too far and used their support as leverage to demand that the offensive behavior change.

Ironically, Wanda feels most judged by her colleagues on the Women of Steel committee, a support and advocacy branch of the USW in which she participates and holds office. At the meetings and events of this committee, she says, "*I feel sometimes I have to downplay myself, especially my appearance. I can't be me as far as my clothes, my gesture—everything—I have to like, soften up, not for the union itself, but for the Women of Steel committee. And as I said, it's very uncomfortable. When we have engagements, I like to dress up, OK? And I am a lesbian. I am the aggressor. I do wear men's clothing. And if we're going out somewhere, I would like to put on my tie, my bow tie, my slacks and everything. It feels like if we were going somewhere I couldn't have this tie on, because they would just look at me, and it's like I shouldn't care what they feel, but it's kinda hard. Then knowing people who have issues with me, it makes it even more hard. I feel like sometimes I'm going to resign because I can't be me. I feel like I can't be me. And it's a battle that I have within myself. And that makes it real hard being a lesbian. An open lesbian, in the union. 'Cause being a regular steel mill worker, union sister, it's no problem. You come in, do your job, get your paycheck and go home. It's no problem.*" Though masculine women are breaking some rules, they are following others, so they can be comfortable and happy at work. In an all-female space, such as Women of Steel meetings, that acceptance disappears and is replaced by disapproval and censure that, while usually unspoken, still do their work of making butch lesbians feel excluded and unwelcome.

Olshana's experience in the mills demonstrates how female masculinity shifts people's interpretation and performance of gender roles. She had no prior mechanical or industrial experience, but took the job as part of a leftist commitment to working with unions and among workers. But once there, she was transformed by the work and her success with it. She remarks, "*I was pretty awestruck by how these guys could fix anything with very few resources. Sometimes to fix something really old they'd have to make a part, or find a part, or scavenge or something. I think that influenced a lot of how I behaved in there because I thought it was so cool that they were able to keep these things, these old things and these big gigantic things, running. And I wanted to be a part of that. It was pretty dramatic seeing these big gigantic glowing billets come in one end of the mill and then see them getting smashed and crushed. Steam, and slag is flying, big banging noises, earth-shaking noises. So these guys, they were doing dangerous and brave things. I was kind of impressed. And I think in the end being involved in something like that tends to flatten out some of the other differences."* Olshana was the only woman in her shanty—the only woman trained as a motor inspector, which is an elite skilled trade within the mill. But she was impressed by her colleagues and strove to be one of them. That dynamic influenced her work experience, and therefore her identity, much more than her gender or sexuality did.

Gail tells a story of a hazing incident that illustrates this process of making femininity invisible. She remembers that *"one of my first jobs was to repair anything wrong with the mine shaft—three thousand feet straight up and down. Replacing timbers, replacing steel beams, just anything that went wrong. You never worked alone. There was always somebody experienced with you. Usually for a job like that there was four of us. And, my first day on the job it was kind of funny, 'cause we worked off the top of the elevator. We'd have the hoistman lower the cage to ground level, and climb on the top of it with our equipment. Railings around it. We had slings and stuff, and timber that we had to replace because the timber gets worn down. And we get down there, probably about level five. And the guys tell me to take the sling and throw it over a beam, and hook a come-along up to it, 'cause we're going to use it to move the beam over in place. So I get out there, and you can't use a safety line with that many people up there, because you get all tangled up. We had to carry them with us, but we never used 'em. And mine was on the top of the cage 'cause I'm climbing out, I don't want to trip on it. And I realize, that's a long drop. So I'm out on this eight-inch-wide steel beam, and I hold on, flip the cable over, and hook up the come-along. All of a sudden the cage takes off, goes down to two levels below. I see it stopping. I'm like, 'Those suckers, I think this is my initiation.' So I very carefully turned around, 'cause now I'm open on both sides of this eight-inch beam, so I turn around and put my back against the beam, and slid down, and sat there, 'cause I didn't know how long I'm going to be there. Probably ten, twelve minutes later I see not only the three guys I'm working with, but there's an extra light on there—turns out it's the general mechanical foreman—and they come up to me and he looks at me and he says 'What the hell are you doing there?' And I looked at the guys and I saw the look of panic on their face—they could have been fired immediately for doing that, 'cause it's endangering somebody's life. And I looked at him and I said, 'They're going for coffee—I don't drink coffee.' He said, 'Get the Hell in here.' After that, I had no problems with at least those guys. They were OK with me. That was my initiation onto the millwright gang."* This gang did not want to work with a woman, but didn't want to work with someone who would betray them to the boss even more. For Gail, this incident illustrates her ability to read the established work culture, and make it work for her. Rather than fight masculine hazing, she fits into it. This strategy both feels good and works well for her.

Gail never explicitly identified herself as a lesbian at work, so her masculine behavior is never specifically linked to sexual orientation in the mill. Yet her lover worked in the same mine she did, and they arranged to be transferred together to the same steel mill when the mine closed. Gail says that she assumes people knew they were lovers—they lived together and openly raised a son—but the words were never spoken. Rather, she carved out a reputation for toughness, humor, and tolerance that earned her the acceptance of co-workers, and comfort with herself. She and her peers found a home for their masculine female identity, defined as doing a job well, meeting and exceeding local standards, and being a welcome member of the work community.

These masculine traits, when they are found in women, stereotypically accompany lesbian identification. Often, lesbians aren't particularly feminine. Often, we are accustomed to harassment and know how to handle it through retaliation and humor. Often, we need to be able to support ourselves and our families independently. Often, we feel comfortable working and socializing with men, because of shared interests and easy assimilation to the culture. This combination of traits also occurs sometimes in straight women, and not all lesbians possess all, or even any, of these traits. Nonetheless, a fortuitous fit between lesbian orientation and steelwork means that many lesbians seek out and thrive in mill jobs, whether they are open about their identity or not.

Wanda summarizes this possibility well. *"When a woman is basically wearing men's clothes, ties, you still get looked at. I know I get looked at a lot. I figure maybe they're jealous because I dress better. I know how to put it together, I study the detail to it."* I respond that she looks good to me, and she grins. *"Yeah, and some men have a problem. Me and my ex-girlfriend, we were walking one night. And she lived up by Randolph up North, and we was walking, it was a guy, and he walked past, and then, y'know when you turn around because you feel like someone's looking? He was looking, and he said, 'You dykes!' Just like that. 'You want to be a man.' I always get that: you want to be a man. It's like, who said I want to be a man? I'm just being me. I don't like labels, first of all. But I know when people have to label me, they're going to have to say, she's a stud, or butch, but other than that, it's just [Wanda], 'cause I'm going to be me. That's just how I look at it—it's just me living my life."*

CHAPTER FIVE

Male Masculinity in the Steel Mill

As discussed in Chapter 4, women who work in the mills are generally perceived as masculine by themselves and others, and they make up an increasingly tiny fraction of current steelworkers. Essentially, then, only men work in basic steel mills, which Nate says that his partner describes as surrounded by *"a green haze of testosterone."* This chapter tells their stories, and draws conclusions about masculinity and gay identity. Though many of its themes also appear in other chapters, here I focus on what it means to be a gay man within a setting in which almost all people are masculine, and virtually no male-bodied people are gay. How does this single-sexed environment affect how masculinity is performed, both at the mill and away from it? We are so accustomed to viewing gender as a binary system, in which each term defines the other as its inverse. The mills provide a unique opportunity to think through what it might mean to escape the tyranny of this binary gender system.

Thus, this chapter presents the stories of twenty men, describing how they experience and inhabit their masculinity in the "man's world" of the mills. Gay men, whose relationship to masculinity is frequently challenged in our culture, negotiate this environment in several different ways. And the range of what mill workers understand as masculine will be relevant. Though female millworkers are few and far between, their masculinity is just as salient as that of their male co-workers. Certainly, that practically all steelworkers are masculine challenges how we tend to view straight men, gay men, lesbians, and even straight women. Everyone's reality gets transformed in an environment in which only one gender can sustain a coherent social system.

Understanding how this single-gender system functions starts with having a detailed, textured picture of what goes on at the mills, and how it feels. Each or my narrators was involved in the production of basic steel in a mill that covered many acres; workers enter past a guard and through a gate into a physically and culturally separate world. James Catano, in his 2001 study of the psychology of American masculinity, focuses on narratives about the steel industry because "it has a longstanding history as a premiere arena for not only rhetorizing masculinity but also enacting masculine values seen as central to—indeed too often equivalent to—national values" (4). Our culture defines what it means to be a man, to be an American, and to be a steelworker by pointing to American male steelworkers.

One paradigmatic example of steely American masculinity is Nate, who repeatedly refers to himself and his former partner as *"bears"* and *"bikers."* Nate is tall and physically imposing, though his jovial demeanor undercuts this effect somewhat. He describes the mill as *"a place where I had to be one of the boys,"* and he jokes that his partner described the mills as surrounded by a *"green haze of testosterone."* To cross into the mills was to enter a different world—one governed by its own rules, and much more remote from its surroundings than mere distance could explain. Christopher Hall, in *Steel Phoenix*, observes that "U.S. steelmakers have traditionally come largely from the most insular region of the country, the Midwest, and from an industry that developed a remarkably insular, almost xenophobic, culture" (207). With minimal exchange between steelworkers and outsiders, with the showering and changing workers do before they leave the mill, with heightened security at entrances, mills remain separate from the culture in which they are situated. And the *"green haze of testosterone"* is both a cause and an effect of that separation. The mill produces masculinity just as it produces steel, and anyone who fits in there both receives and generates that message.

Jay, who has a drinking problem but had been sober for five months when we met, hides his gay identity at work because he's scared of retaliation from his co-workers and of being laid off, since globalization leads him to feel expendable. Like so many other steelworkers, he feels vulnerable from multiple directions and experiences this vulnerability as a challenge to his masculinity. Jay has been married to women, has been in long-term relationships with men, and has had numerous casual sexual encounters with men, both at work and elsewhere. Looking back over his life, he feels loneliness and isolation competing with fear of discovery. He'd like to stop hiding at work, since he says it was the stress of maintaining that deception that led him to alcohol. But he doesn't feel safe, since he believes that both the company and the union are *"a bunch of redneck guys, good ol' boys' club, yes ma'am. I'm telling you, I'd be the laughing stock. It's sad. It's terrible. We're lucky we even got jobs. And then this guy from the Middle East, this Axelor Mittal, you think he's going to support homosexuality? In his country, they kill you for being gay. . . . They're all from the Middle East. In them countries, they kill you for being gay. In Cuba, they lock you up and torture you for being gay. I guess it ain't so bad over here. I don't understand why it's wrong to feel something for an individual, male or female, that you just actually feel love for someone in a way that you want to spend your life with 'em. I just want to be with someone."* Here, Jay is linking lack of protection for gay workers to the economic crisis (*"we're lucky we even have jobs"*) and to globalization. Everyone in the mill fears layoffs and feels at the mercy of global power shifts. Jay is misinformed about the nature of foreign involvement (Lakshmi Mittal is from India, and Arcelor is a Belgian conglomerate—there is no connection between ArcelorMittal and the Middle East), but what's important is that he does not attribute his fear of reprisal if his sexual preference became known at work to his co-workers or to company or federal policy. Instead, he blames it on economic pressures that make him glad to have a job at any cost and interference from foreigners whose countries are even more antigay than ours.

Understanding the culture of the mills—the sense of being beleaguered, unappreciated, and under threat from vague, external forces—is crucial to understanding how masculinity works in the mill. Since self-presentation tends to be reactive (in a context, motivated by change or opposition), the exaggerated, exclusive performance of masculinity in the mills may be a response to threats, real or imagined, from African Americans, women, foreign investors, job loss, and gay men. As Mary Margaret Fonow notes, since big steel was linked to masculinity and to the United States' rise to world prominence, the collapse of the steel industry "became a metaphor not only for decline and decay but also for the loss of manhood" (22). When this collapse occurs, who gets blamed, who pays the price, and how does masculinity reconstitute itself?

The mills, and what happens within them, have not changed much over the last hundred years; both the current process and its culture emerged early in the twentieth century. As Carol Olson reports, in *Steel Wives*, mill labor created "harsh, unhealthy, often dangerous conditions, contributing to a masculine environment of both camaraderie and competitiveness" (36). Dave describes his work in the blast furnace by saying, *"To me, it's like working on a volcano."* He explains the process of continuous casting, and the working conditions it creates. *"You could not, under no circumstances, get up to that level, so it's always an emergency, you've got to get these tap-holes opened up. . . . So you try to stop the molten iron and many times we missed. Can you imagine a thing of iron maybe ten feet long and maybe 150 feet acrost, and the wind is just pushing it?"* Dave is here trying to convey a sense of the scale, the danger, and the stress of his job day-to-day. And it's hard to explain to an outsider. His desire to share these experiences is thwarted by their alien nature, by his incomplete knowledge of the big picture, and by a lack of vocabulary comprehensible to the uninitiated.

Isabel, who has worked on a mill janitorial crew doing mundane tasks not directly related to the production of steel, describes her father, a long-time mill worker whose persona reinforces this masculine creed: *"Steel-workers got to be big, they got to be tough, they got to be strong. The work they do is not for what you would consider a sissy or anything like that. My dad is a vet, manly guy, likes his football. He's polite, he's a gentleman but he can blow a fuse right off the bat due to years of being undermined at his work. How they were treated up at the steel mills too, they're always thinking about who's the toughest one, we've got to pick the toughest ones. The pictures you see of the steel mills, you think of some big, tough, strong, burly guy, and it'd be really weird if someone took off their welding mask and it was a girl, they'd be like 'unh unh, that's not right.' It's so embedded in your mind that it has to be a guy, and it has to be strong, and it has to be straight."* Isabel gives voice to the connection between her father's being undermined at work, his anger, and women's exclusion. If being a steelworker no longer guarantees masculinity since layoffs, give-backs, corporate takeovers and negative media attention all collude to make even those steelworkers with jobs feel insecure and defensive, then steelworker masculinity must be reinforced through the exclusion of women and gay men.

Yet this exclusion is a challenge, since masculinity is often reinforced through sexual language or behavior between men, which often resembles the behavior it purports to exclude. Esther Newton notes, in her 1972 ethnology *Mother Camp*, that "the middle-class idea tends to be that any man who has had sexual relations with men is queer [while] . . . lower-class men give themselves a bit more leeway before they consider themselves to be gay" (102). Though this provocative statement appears in a footnote, and Newton makes no attempt to prove or explain it there, she subsequently observes that, from her middle-class perspective, working-class norms of masculinity and femininity seem exaggerated—even idealized. For working-class people, "the only 'real' men look like football tackles, act at all times like John Wayne, and are 'hung like stud mules.' At base, 'masculinity' is the principle of aggressive brute force in the world" (127). Among blue-collar workers, masculinity is exaggerated, old-fashioned, and compulsory. At any rate, it seems that way to outsiders.

Like Newton, I am a middle-class researcher, trying to understand a gender system whose codes are alien. I've spent countless nights in working-class gay bars discussing my research with the regulars, trolling for steelworkers. They have reminded me, both directly and indirectly, of Newton's first point—if I limit myself to steelworkers who identify themselves as gay, I exclude many folks who have experiences that I would consider gay. Ian notes that, just out of high school, he learned that he was gay by hanging out with steelworkers who weren't: *"You'd have to watch out for this guy who'd come up behind you and give you the bum rub <chuckles>. You'd have to be careful about certain men, you'd have to bend over and all this ridiculous teasing—so very much homophobic banter, but on the other hand very homoerotic themes there as well, too, because there were all these guys there. So that was one of those themes that sort of influenced my sexuality as I got older."* The mill context—exclusively masculine, working-class, physical—makes possible for all men pleasures that would, in another context, be limited to gay men. Rather than try to differentiate between male-male sexual behavior and gay identity, I here relate the steelworker's stories about how it works for them—how sexuality and gender take shape, and what masculinity means, as it unfolds in an exclusively masculine context.

Nate describes his initial experiences with this system in which masculinity gets established through male-male sexual play. *"There was a lot of horseplay. Tons and tons of horseplay. I tell you, it was basically a gay man's paradise because you could be gay and open probably and no one would ever know as long as you didn't take it too terribly far. There was a lot of ass-slapping and various different things in the showers. My very first day there, I thought I would be doing the whole steelworker thing, and I was taking a shower. I was twenty years old, not nearly as heavy as I am now, and probably a lot better looking than I am now with my white hair. I was washing my face, and all of a sudden it was 1, 2, 3, 4, there was two hands on my genitals, and two hands on my face. The two hands on my face were mine. It's like, OK, I don't remember having two extra hands. It's extremely hard to be tough when you're naked, young, and [have] soap in your eyes, but I did kind of indicate to the gentleman that decided he needed to help me with my shower that I was going to break his arm off and put it in his butt, and he just kind of laughed and of course everybody else was laughing and it was my initiation into the steel mill. But plenty of the guys were OK with that kind of stuff. It was like, 'Here, let me help you with that' and stuff. There was a lot of penis envy. There were a couple of the guys that were quite well developed, and they didn't mind, y'know letting others look and/or touch. There was that kind of play. . . . I think it's a little bit like the old West. A lot of the guys were very testosterone charged. . . . I say, it's kind of like working at a candy store. The first week you've got to try all the candy, or at least take a look at it all, and then after all it's just like, it's candy, and you just have to go on."* This horseplay didn't fit his initial expectation—when he thought he'd *"be doing the whole steelworker thing,"* he imagined masculinity as precluding male-male sexual contact. What he found in practice was more consistent with his gay identity, though profoundly unfriendly to acknowledgement of queer desire. So his response is to compartmentalize sex and desire, concluding *"it's candy, and you just have to go on."*

Nate is not the only steelworker who describes a work environment replete with horseplay and male-male sexual contact or near contact; all the male steelworkers describe ribald, aggressive sexual exchanges between men at work. Even those like Keith, who stop short of *"fooling around"* at work, note that men *"run around whack each other's asses and stuff like that. It's a very different kind of atmosphere, in the shower. Like I said before, they're all kind of perverted, they go around making sexual innuendos with each other, a lot of times the worst is when you're in the shower. It's just a very weird atmosphere. It's hard to explain when it comes to that part."* And Chris reports *"messing around near the mill, sometimes AT the mill, sometimes at their house when their wife wasn't there, or at my house when no one was around."* His casual mention of these men's wives reflects a common pattern: the sexual encounters my narrators report involve straight men. Those I interviewed typically present themselves as straight at work, and their partners are married straight men. Yet Chris concludes, *"More than I came on to came on to me, which was interesting."* Though he identifies as a gay man in nonwork settings, he is not the main initiator of male-male sex he has had at the mill.

Andy is among the most frank about sexual encounters in the mill. He says it's very common; for him, it's rare for a week to go by without some sort of sex at work, and he describes his partners as married straight men who want to *"get him off."* He quips that *"it's all about eye contact. Just the other day I was at work, just doing my job, when a co-worker caught my eye, and then headed to the men's room. I waited a few minutes, then followed him in there. When I went into a stall, he knelt down and got right to it. Pretty soon, he swallowed my load, and we went right back to work."* Scott says he worked with a man called Dixie, and that *"everyone knew that he was gay because he advertised it, and he carried a purse. Colored fellow. Beautiful body, I mean he was built. He was like a state champ wrestler, I guess, in high school. And he loved his guys and he would take them orally or otherwise, one after another.*

All over the mill. There's more beds in the mill than you would ever believe. They had some pretty good accommodations."

Fred suggested I interview him, after his day shift, in a local restaurant, where he didn't eat anything, though he smoked continuously. He says he's had sex with countless men in the mill. *"In fact that day I had called you I had sex in the mill. I have a regular. I had two regulars. And when I was sober for a long time, the black guy regular, he drank so much, I could taste alcohol in his cum, and I finally got tired of getting a mouth full of alcohol and I said I can't do this anymore and I cut him off,"* and he laughs and shrugs. When Fred transferred to a new department, he says a new co-worker came up and asked, *"Is it true you're gay? I said yeah, he said, 'Want to suck my dick?' I said, sure, and we snuck off in the pit somewhere. In my old department we called this one guy number 7 because he was going to be my seventh. And they were correct—I had had sex with six guys in that department, and I don't know how they knew that, I really don't."* The sexual braggadocio in stories like this one are a reminder that narrators may exaggerate or fabricate stories. Still, there's enough similarities among the accounts of men who do not know each other, and are surprised to hear that other gay steelworkers exist, to make the general climate of frequent male-male sex at work believable.

Xena confirms this description by commenting, off the cuff, that *"There's a lot of drinking, a lot of sex out there. One time I truly walked in on two men. I walked into a storage room, and I saw these two guys going at it. I said, 'Sorry' <sheepishly> and I thought, if they had the lights off no one would have known. It was locked. But about an hour later I saw one of them and said, 'Sorry, but you're secret's safe with me.' He was very—there's a lot of that out there. The pretty boys, always dressing nice."*

Some of the most interesting research on working-class masculinity comes out of Australia, where R. W. Connell, M. D. Davis, and G. W. Dowsett (in a chapter they contributed to Connell's *The Men and the Boys*) study how "conditions of working-class life affect sexuality" (103). They observe that, since many working-class jobsites are single-sex and monotonous, smut, ribaldry, and sex are common there (108). They identify "a continuum of homoerotic experience among working-class men in a number of social settings. At the same time we must acknowledge that the experience is silenced" (109) due to traditional family ideology and accompanying gender roles, and to masculinity's link to physical prowess. The erotic practice they trace is "generally masturbatory or oral-genital, not often anal" (114), which their research subjects believe belongs in gay, long-term relationships. Recent research on U.S. masculinities, such as E. Patrick Johnson's account of black gay men in the South, has much in common with this Australian research. Several of Johnson's narrators are in straight marriages or live straight lives, and their simultaneous male-male sexual behavior, like that of southerners in general, is "allowable as long as the indiscretion is not flaunted" (4). Thus, to participate in same-sex sexual behavior does not require identification as a gay person, nor does it generate acceptance of gay folks or gay choices. This disjuncture is observed by many of my narrators, including Jay, who notes with incredulity, *"They're doing straight guys. Gay guys doing straight guys, y'know?"*

In a context where sex that could be described as gay is both widespread and condemned, how do self-identified gay men see themselves and their masculinity? Jay is very articulate about this: *"There's so many times I want to say something, I'm a very outspoken person. And I know I can't and I want to and I'm so angry and so mad and sometimes I don't know what I am."* Lonely and scared, Jay wants to be honest with his co-workers, many of whom are close friends whom he feels bad about deceiving, and he wants to find a stable, loving relationship. *"But I have to live a lie because I don't know how safe I am, and I live in a country that won't tell me how safe I am."* Lack of a clear identity and fear of the unknown characterize not only gay men, but all men in the mills, since they're all trying to establish masculinity within a single-gender system.

For these steelworkers, the process of establishing and maintaining masculinity is complicated by stereotypes about and within the working class, and by shifts within the gay liberation movement. Appleby's ethnographic study of nine working-class gay men concludes that "gender role conformity" (63) is required for survival in blue-collar jobs. Embrick, Walther, and Wickens agree that gay people in working-class settings use traditional gender roles as a means of avoiding detection. They note that blue-collar workplaces appear more accepting of difference than they once were, but that this change remains on the level of policy only—overt discrimination is still the norm in practice. Relentless homophobic comments, and even violence, work to "sustain rigid boundaries around masculinity and are frequently utilized to create a white working-class male solidarity based on the perseverance of heteronormativity" (765). Working-class men, then, are masculine in self-defense.

Yet at the same time, gay men are culturally defined as gender-role nonconforming. Esther Newton gives a history of the formation of a specifically gay identity, noting that: "The identity or paradigm of a special kind of person, a despised effeminate man who desires *only* other men or a masculine woman with the complimentary inclination, is rooted in the origins of the modern worldview which first emerged in the West during the eighteenth century" (*Cherry Grove* 10). She then observes that Cherry Grove, Fire Island—the first place dominated and controlled by people who identified as gay—cemented "the image or paradigm of what it meant to be gay, the (false) idea that gay is synonymous with young, white, male, promiscuous, artistically inclined, and middle-class" (11). Steelworkers are not included within this stereotype, by virtue of both class and related limitations on gender-role nonconforming behavior (i.e. you can't be feminine in a steel mill). As a consequence, steelworkers are unable to access their culture's dominant symbols and representations of gayness. Gay male steelworkers can't make themselves visible to themselves and to others in the usual ways because of the masculinity required by their class identity.

Like many working-class gays, my narrators often scorn the urban gay scene as exemplified by pride parades and "boys' town" nightlife. They don't feel included or welcome in this milieu and credit its extremism and self-satisfaction with making their struggles to achieve acceptance harder. Jay explains that *"to me, being gay doesn't mean you run around and throw it in somebody's face,"* and Dave observes that *"there's nothing wrong with being out, and we should be proud of it, but I don't think we should be literally rubbing it in people's faces either, because you run the risk of alienating people who do support you. But some people are drama queens, and some people, you wouldn't be able to pick them out in a crowd. Most people's image of gays have always been the carnival, the gay pride thing, where there's drag, with next to no clothes on, and it's a stereotype, and we're starting to break that. There are these levels of respect in our society. You've got to be an accepted person, but when you're doing everything in your power to turn people against you . . . Some people are not gay, they work hard at being gay. All life is about primping in front of a mirror—I could care less. I'm going to get out there and do what I've got to do, and damn everybody."* His rejection of the stereotypical urban gay lifestyle is about class and privilege more than femininity. Dave wants *"respect"* and *"to get out there and do what I've got to do"*—for him, effectiveness trumps self-expression, represented by *"drama queens"* and people with *"next to no clothes on."*

My narrators' objections to urban manifestations of gayness are, in part, a response to the cultural assumption that to be urban is the only way to be gay—that anyone not living in a big city should move there as part of the coming-out process. Obviously, plenty of queers choose to stay away from big cities, and don't adopt the behaviors and codes associated with urban gay life. And my narrators resent being judged marginal, or not gay enough, for making that choice. Worth noting is that, as Scott Herring insists in his book *Another Country*, the distinction between the rural and the urban is "as much phantasmatic as it is factual," since "space and place are as much act and experience as they are dirt and rock, concrete and steel" (13). Northwest Indiana is urban, yet the lives of the steelworkers are at a mental and temporal distance from urban mentalities or aesthetics. They express this by mocking the urban gay scene, and also by being a part of it, by adapting and adopting some of its styles and techniques.

For example, the men I interviewed called my attention to their femininity in various ways. Nate cooked me an elaborate meal and led me through his beautiful house, noting that *"I'm a well-rounded gay man. I can build the house, and then decorate it."* Dave described his antiquing strategies, and his early decision to sink his time and money into art and into improving his house. Jay joked, *"I'm no different from anybody else. I have the same aspirations. A little frillier, but . . ."* He notes that *"I have my moments of femininity,"* which he finds evidence of in his carefully kept, though tiny, apartment: *"Now you look at my house. There's not too many guys that have a house done up like this. Most gay men are like that. True."* Later, he clarifies, *"I'm not feminine. I have my moments. I guess I show some signs of it, I guess. But it's not something I practice, it's not something I just openly do."* It's as though, to see himself as a gay man, each marks himself as feminine, while simultaneously downplaying this trait. It's then a simple matter to excise femininity at work, since it's largely discursive anyway.

These interlocking, contradictory practices complicate claiming gay male identity as a steelworker. The dominant, recognizable ways of being gay exclude yet fetishize working-class men. Andy notes wryly that *"boys clubs are packed with men in Wolverines,"* referring to a brand of steel-toed work boots, yet these same men wouldn't be willing *"to drive by my plant, let alone work there."* While the men I interviewed all identify as gay, what that means to them is less clear. When they call urban middle-class gay people spoiled, silly children, they're staking claim to a different kind of gay male masculinity. Nate claims, *"I'm a very butch gay boy, but I bring out my effeminate side if I choose. I'm not totally what I would call rough and tumble but I am a manly man."*

Steelworker in front of Bessemer stacks,
ca. 2006. Photograph by A. K. MacGrew.

Jay Clarkson has done research on gay masculinity as seen on the web-site StraightActing.com, which he describes as an ongoing struggle to see who can be the most masculine. But working-class masculinity is involved in this struggle only symbolically: according to Clarkson, some gay men choose a working-class aesthetic in their quest for hypermasculinity (192). But here the working-class aesthetic is just a costume that members of this online community use to distance themselves from the feminized gay identity they find distasteful. Clarkson's research doesn't concern actual working-class men, but it does add another layer to our understanding of gay steelworker's relationship to masculinity.

Presumably, the steelworkers who responded to my invitations, con-tacted me, and signed consent forms are more gay-identified than those I did not speak to. Nan Alamilla Boyd believes that oral historians should learn from queer and feminist theorists that the process of disclosing one's self produces, rather than merely reveals, identity. By soliciting stories from gay people, she suggests, I limit myself to those gay people who embrace gay identity with some degree of pride, and I exclude queer desires and behaviors that don't fit this model (183). Though aware of these limitations, I focus on how people who identify as gay mesh this self with their work identity. These two identities seem mutually exclusive: there are no gay steelworkers, and gay people are not members of the working class. What is it like to occupy that nonexistent overlap?

Masculinity, Queerness, and Steel All Involve Risk-Taking

The mill is a place that depends on the production of masculinity, yet at the same time, frequent sex between men is one behavior that makes masculinity difficult to establish, as does the absence of femininity. Jay links the difficult working environment to the absence of women, noting that he can't be open about his sexual preference because *"I have commitments. People expect things from me. Sometimes I think I'm going to go somewhere and just go away, change my name, and lose myself and never come back. I love Hawaii, I've never been there, but I just love it. I'm on probation, but I don't think I'm a bad person, I think that I'm depressed and lonely, and my job makes me more depressed and lonely. The steel mill is a hard place to work, it's a harsh, harsh environment. Everyone expects you to be macho. You're supposed to be like a rough biker. You're not supposed to show your emotions, you're not supposed to cry. Anyone who's anybody drinks as far as the steel mill is concerned. The problem out there now is there's very few women. This guy, he basically made it almost all white men. He gives out applications and tells you to ask a family member and all these guys ask guys. And he gets away with it for that reason. Very few minorities out there now. The women I work with though, if you didn't know they were women, you'd swear they were men. They are very, very manly. They are hard-core, buddy. They'd call the preacher to drink. Very hard-core women. And I only work with two or three of them."* By Jay's logic, since there are few women in the mills, and those few are very masculine, femininity doesn't get expressed in mill culture, which leaves no space available in which to be a gay man.

Gay male steelworkers don't define themselves in contrast with women, since women in the mill are scarce and as masculine as they are, and they don't define themselves as part of a gay community "given the class composition of the emerging inner-city gay community and the reaction of significant numbers of [working-class] men against the commercial scene" (Connell 123). Thus, they tend to define themselves through risk-taking behavior. Male steelworkers, regardless of sexuality, rely on dangerous, difficult work to establish their masculinity, and gay men may simply do so with a little more desperation. According to Connell, what is defined as men's work is also the most dangerous, including work involving pollution

(187). Working-class men have only one asset to market, their body's capacity to labor, "and their bodies are, over time, consumed by the labor they do" (187). Class and work are thus directly linked to life expectancy and health outcomes. "Given these conditions, working men may embrace the process that consumes their bodies, as their way of 'doing' masculinity, and claiming some self-respect in the damaging world of wage labor" (188).

Scott, for example, takes obvious pride in the danger of mill work, and links both that danger and his pride to toughness and masculinity. *"We used chloroethane in the mill when I was first in the slabber in the 70s, we washed in it because it cleaned good, we washed our greens in it 'cause it cleaned good, and we'd hang the greens over the blower, which dried great, but blew the fumes everywhere. All the pipes were covered with asbestos. We would pull the asbestos off to reach the pipes. Benzene was all over the mill. And everything that comes off the hot metal from the blast furnace, or the BOF, we're breathing these fumes. I think in most cases the human body has a lot of tolerance. God really built us good to handle all this shit that we've done. When you read all about the picky, picky environmental stuff that we have now. One billionth part per billion. We used to chew on it."*

As Deborah Rudacille observes in her study of the Sparrows Point mill, *Roots of Steel*, "Retired steelworkers suffer from a broad range of health conditions directly related to their employment, even apart from life-threatening diseases like cancer" (138). Though workers are usually aware of the short- and long-term health effects of their jobs, the high pay outweighs the danger for them. Furthermore, Rudacille quotes workers stating that "in the coke ovens, 'a kind of macho attitude prevailed' . . . with workers doing whatever they had to do to get the job done" (139). The mills and the government could get away with minimal safety enforcement because workers, rather than demanding increased safety, often resisted improvements as part of their attempt to seem masculine, daring, and free.

Lakisha, who worked as a safety inspector, observes that steelworker masculinity depends, at least in part, on a refusal of safety measures and an embrace of risk. She observes that *"a lot of guys would just be stubborn and they wouldn't want to wear their protective clothes."* When she did rounds asking for input from other workers about safety hazards, she found that *"they were actually more inclined to approach you if I walked in by myself and their buddies weren't watching them. They'd be like, hey, y'know, this could be a lot better."* When other men are present, steelworkers strive to be tough and uninterested in safety, but that persona can be relaxed when they are alone or when only women are present.

When my narrators discuss risks and health effects, they do so in a very matter-of-fact manner, and they juxtapose the discussion with comments about pay rates. Nate, for example, describes dramatic situations in a calm, noncommittal way. *"The areas I worked in was drawing and galvanizing fabric. [In] the drawing department there was a lot of dust because our lubrications were a powder-type lube. They looked like soap detergent, like what you do your laundry with. It was a combination of lime and animal fat. It would powder up so there'd be a lot of dust in the air. The galvanizing department originally used lead, zinc. . . . Lead poisoning was very prevalent. The temperature of the zinc was about 850 degrees. Lead furnaces were about 1800. It was very, very hot. We switched over, which was a little bit more environmentally friendly, to fluidized beds, which was a combination of air jets, gas jets, and sand that moved to actually scrub the lubrications off the wire before it went through the zinc to be galvanized. Again, they were 1800 to 2,000 degrees. I had to look into those, and I kept a permanent tan. My face, and I always wear my shirt kind of open, those areas were always tan year round, and basically I was cooking my skin. I was being baked."* He follows this account with the comment: *"I enjoyed my work at the steel mill. I need to let the world know that. It wasn't the most fulfilling job I've ever had, but I did enjoy it. It was the best-paying job I've ever had."* Though he has described, in an informed, dispassionate tone, chemical damage to his face and neck, the job still feels important and enjoyable to him (as well as lucrative), and these qualities take precedence.

Keith, a gunner, describes the health risks in a brief, to-the-point manner. *"The spray is ambient in the air. There's a lot of cancer-causing chemicals. There's a lot of guys with cancer. They don't wear respirators, because it's so hot in there, they would catch fire. They just try not to breathe right then. The ambient air temperature is about 500 degrees. When I gun the furnace, I move this big pipe in—it's more than 50 pounds, and I'm holding the very end of it. So I'm in a very hot environment, wearing layers and layers of safety gear, exerting myself. It's very hard to describe. This is a young person's job. I weighed 270 when I started this job. Now I weigh just under 200. It just melts off you. When I get off the job and go upstairs, I can hardly get my clothes off. They're just soaking. I'm the lowest-paid job at the mill. I make $19.79 an hour. When I get promoted, I'll make $21.78 an hour."* He concludes: *"I'm just a high school graduate. There's nowhere else in the world that I could make this much money that I'm making now."* Keith is a younger man than the other narrators, and he doesn't even pretend that there aren't extreme environmental health risks to his job, but those risks are almost a source of pride to him.

He describes them with an offhand, romanticized casualness. This attitude crops up often in accounts of mill life by (presumably) straight steelworkers. Wymard quotes men who associate the "romance of the mill" with the excitement provided by danger and death. One eighteen-year-old worker liked "to be around all that hot stuff, especially when walking on top of it, it burned your legs. For a kid, the mill was an exciting place to be. But it was risky. You could be killed" (20). The mystique of mill work derives from its danger and the chance to flirt with death.

Miles lists negative health effects with calm articulateness. *"You're surrounded by silicosis, you're surrounded by products that will give you mesothelioma, it's prevalent. They do not put warning labels on the materials, 'cause I've looked for 'em. What ingredients are in here? They're not going to tell you. So you're subject to it, because of all the dust. It's not a perfect place. The pay is good, I'm going to say that. For someone that would walk out with just a high school diploma the pay is good, definitely the pay is there."* Though officially the money is what makes it worth it, the risks in and of themselves are also kind of sexy.

When I asked about health effects, people would tell me isolated stories, such as Gail's account: *"I got in on the ground floor of a hot tip line. We worked with chromium and chromate and stuff like that. We had a lot of carcinogens. And yeah they give you protective equipment, but by the time you had it on you could've had the job done and over with, so a lot of times you got sprayed with it anyways. I would be careful—if I got sprayed I washed it off."* Other narrators as well spoke of the dangerous choices they made, both to work in the mill and to select specific jobs within it, that were justified by the need to earn a living. In all of these comments, what's striking is the sense of pride and satisfaction that comes from describing the danger and risk involved. Fear is what makes the job exciting, thrilling, cool.

Phil describes the risks of his job as a caster, noting that *"not where I work but in other castors there have been fatalities, where things that were supposed to work a certain way just don't. We depend a lot on water—we cool everything down by water. If we lose our water, the steel doesn't set up right, and then it just starts flying everywhere, so there's a lot of human error and mechanical error that could go wrong. If we lose all our water, we create a hydrogen bomb, we're just basically sitting in a hydrogen bomb, all the steam inside where the water's supposed to be, will just superheat to the point where it all is just forced to explode."* Though the job itself is not that hard, the risk of what could happen if things go wrong, and the image of what a steelworker looks and acts like, creates and reinforces a macho persona. Phil claims that I could

Work crew, Inland Steel, East Chicago, late 1970s.
Courtesy of the Calumet Regional Archives.

learn his job in just a few months, offering my presumed competence as evidence that you don't have to be big and strong like him, yet he says that most people he tries to recruit *"don't see themselves working out there."* This decision is not *"because of the sweat and the cold and the nasty stuff I have to go through"* but just because they don't identify with the burly, aggressive image they associate with steelworkers. He can't understand why this objection trumps the high pay in their minds, but he does see why people believe they wouldn't fit in, and couldn't succeed.

The gay male steelworkers I interviewed are, at least in part, trying to fill these shoes—they want to play the part scripted for them by our culture. And the part fits them well or they wouldn't persist; they enjoy the work, their co-workers, the diminished but still tangible respect of the community, the high pay, and the majesty. At the same time, they see themselves as part of the subculture of gay men, and they identify with that role when possible. The overlap between these two roles—the cultural impossibility of embodying both gay male and working-class masculinity—creates a friction by which masculinity in general gets shifted and shaped. Consider the popularity in the United States of the film and musical *Billy Elliot*, which tells two intersecting stories: that of a coal miners' strike in England in the early 1980s and that of a boy who realizes his talent in ballet. Why these two stories together? First, it's the *boy* who is good at ballet. All the town girls are awkward and dorky, so when a boy shows up accidentally, the instructor is thrilled, volunteers huge amounts of her time to coach him privately, and leads him eventually to the Royal Ballet. Meanwhile, the miners' strike is going badly, since Margaret Thatcher is leading the country away from what the miners see as its cooperative, folksy, working-class roots, which creates a need for a new, more appropriate model of masculinity. Billy develops that model through reference to girls (the ballet), to gay men (his best friend Michael, a "poof"), and to working-class traditions. Songs about unions ("We're proud to be working class—solidarity forever" says one chorus) parallel songs validating self-expression sung by little boys in dresses. These two inconsistent narratives—of the working-class man and the gay man—combine to redefine masculinity for the twenty-first century.

The role of sex in this process is complicated. Our culture tends to respond with embarrassing enthusiasm to accounts of male-male sex between folks in minority groups. When the term "the down low" (by which African American men describe a continuum of male-male sexual behavior coexisting with heterosexual identification) infiltrated the media and academic culture, it generated interest far out of proportion with the actual occurrence of the behavior it described. When I discuss sex between male steelworkers, both straight- and gay-identified, I become part of such a process, but with the intent of understanding and interpreting behavior such as sex between men in the mills in a cultural and historical context.

The historian George Chauncey identifies a parallel pattern in the behavior of gay men in early twentieth-century New York. Chauncey believes that our modern, post-Stonewall, mostly middle-class sense of what it means to be gay affects what we see when we examine the sexual behavior of other generations or other classes. Specifically, he thinks that we call a person gay if that person engages in (or wishes for) something that we would define as gay sex. Yet his research shows that in turn-of-the-twentieth-century New York, men were considered "normal" (what we call "straight") even if they had frequent sexual encounters with other men. Gender presentation, rather than the sex of one's romantic or sexual partner, determined masculinity. In particular, working-class men "alternated between male and female sexual partners without believing that interest in one precluded interest in the other, or that their occasional recourse to male sexual partners, in particular, indicated an abnormal, 'homosexual,' or even 'bisexual' disposition" (65). This "sexual ideology," not predicated on the sharp hetero/homo divide that seems inevitable today, "had particular efficacy in organizing the sexual practices of men in the social milieu in which it might be least expected: in the highly aggressive and quintessentially 'masculine' subculture of young and usually unmarried sailors, common laborers, hoboes, and other transient workers" (65). Chauncey points out that unstigmatized sexual behavior between men persisted much longer in working-class culture than it did in middle-class culture, yet even in working-class, ethnic contexts, it was gone by the mid-1900s. This, then, might be one more way in which the steel mills resist change. They are hypermasculine, working-class enclaves where at least some aspects of the early twentieth-century permission to have sex with men (as long as you look and feel very masculine) persists.

Another commonality between the steelworkers and the early twentieth-century working-class men described by Chauncey is the role of oral sex. Norman is one of many steelworkers who told me that straight men sought out *"blow jobs in the mill because their wives wouldn't give that to 'em."* And Norman goes on to say that these blow jobs would be provided by female mill laborers or office workers and by male mill workers as well. Chauncey claims that feminine men (he uses the contemporary term "fairies") and prostitutes "engaged in certain forms of sexual behavior, particularly oral sex, which many working-class and middle-class women alike rejected as unbecoming to a woman, 'dirty' and 'perverted'" (61). Getting a blow job from another man at work doesn't make you gay—it just makes you someone who likes blow jobs, searching for a convenient means to get them. As Jay says, *"Some of those biker guys that work out there, they're just very hard-core. But what's funny is a lot of those straight guys they have no problem with getting their dicks sucked, they don't think there's anything wrong with that."*

Though the parallels are many and fascinating, the steelworkers I interviewed are also different from the New Yorkers Chauncey researched. The chief difference is their secrecy. Because the men Chauncey studied were not considered queer as long as they acted masculine, they didn't conceal their male-male sexual practices, and in fact often bragged about them. By contrast, not a single straight-identified male steelworker I spoke to casually referenced sexual encounters with other men at work, though the accounts I got from gay workers suggest that many of them participate. Though I only spoke informally to whatever straight male steelworkers I happened into conversation with (since they were not part of my research process), none that I asked admitted to having sex with other men at work. They seemed horrified by the question. Which is, of course, the point. In the twenty-first century, such behavior would label them as gay, which is a label that very few steelworkers are prepared to take on.

Of the few men I interviewed who are out at work, Fred is the most flamboyant. He has long fingernails painted a glittery red. He had touched them up between work and our interview and had to let them dry thoroughly before he could pick up a pen to sign the consent form. He has long, teased and feathered hair, and wears many earrings in each ear, some of which are long and feathery. And his mannerisms are very queeny. He engages in showy jokes, often at his own expense, that involve exaggerated hand gestures. He lisps. Fred notes that he uses this flamboyance as a form of self-defense. *"They can't say anything about me that I haven't said already. They can't accuse me of anything that I don't put out there myself. They don't bother criticizing me, because, what would be the point? They know they can count on me, and that I'm being honest, and they respect that."* Rosy as this sounds, Fred has been in and out of alcohol rehab centers all across the country (at mill expense), though he proudly noted, at the time of our interview, that he had been clean and sober for seven months. And he showed me a photo, taken on his cell phone, of graffiti at his jobsite that says DIE FAG DIE, suggesting that even in an environment where he feels relative acceptance, there is stress, fear, and hardship. Several narrators compare the mills to a prison setting, or to combat situations. The danger, the physical exertion, and the cooperation between (mostly) men changes the rules in ways that are not new, but that shift how we understand the construction of gay identity.

Miles began working in a steel mill in 1999 as an out lesbian, but he quit about eight years later because of repeated shoulder injuries and general exhaustion. He says it's not really accurate to say that he transitioned while working at the mill, since *"we never really have a transition. We'll always be transgendered because our past experiences and history go along with us. So I'll always consider myself transitioning."* I met Miles at the Cornwall Iron Furnace just outside of Philadelphia. It's a National Historic Landmark, preserving a nineteenth-century ironmaking complex and documenting the ironmaking process, as well as its effect on the area around the furnace and the workers' lives. Miles had suggested this meeting place, noting that he had always wanted to see the exhibits. He was curious about the history of the steelmaking process, and tickled by seeing his huge, powerful, masculine job echoed within this seemingly fragile incarnation made of bricks, and described for us by local elderly ladies.

For example, once the iron in Cornwall was molten, it was poured into one central branch, from which it flowed into a row of troughs pressed into the sand, which we were told resembled baby pigs nursing a sow—hence the name "pig iron." Miles noted that his job used many of the same techniques, since *"I was a spruer. Parts will come out of a didion* [a brand of metal separating equipment], *which shook off the sand, and my job was to break the pieces apart. You see them come out on that long bar, they were lying them into them troughs, that's called a sprue tree, OK, as it goes down along, now in modern times, we have machines that press sand blocks together if you're working on small parts. 'Cause we don't work on really big stuff, we work on couplings so it was smaller stuff. It would come down and this didion would spin it around, and little stars inside would clean off the material, but it still wasn't fully clean. It put them down on this table, which would shake up and down, and they were split in half, and the stuff would go and be remelted and what we wanted to keep for good pieces would go down and be cleaned and checked. I would stand there with a lead hammer and whack those pieces off the sprue tree. Separate the sprue tree from the good stuff."* Seeing the shape of the sprue tree pressed into sand on the floor in front of a gigantic, prehistoric ladle made this whole process more comprehensible to me. And though the scale was much smaller than that of the big production mills still in operation, it was nonetheless vast—the blast furnace was about three stories high, with tap holes at the bottom from which the finished product ran.

The human component of steelmaking similarly remains fairly constant. After we examined a replica of a nineteenth-century steelworker dressed for work, Miles showed me his respirator, noting *"The kerchief on the man's face? This would be more of a modern version of the kerchief."* He also showed me his leather apron, adding that *"they still use the [wooden] shoes, by the way. Nothing has really gotten up to date I guess you'd say. It's really an old art form. I would call it an art form."* His burn clothes are made of Kevlar but otherwise duplicate the old patterns. This continuity is part of the cultural and historical context crucial to understanding how masculinity gets defined and shifted within the mills. The work remains the same, even though the larger culture's definitions of gender and masculinity are shifting. Countless published accounts document the struggles of steelworker families when the man of the house is laid off and the woman has to find work. Though this shift occurred well after second-wave feminism, when most American women were in the paid workforce, the consistency of steelwork, and the corollary consistency of steelworkers' gender roles, made it hard for these families to adjust.

Miles attributes his fascination with the consistency of mill work and mill workers over time to his experience with occupying both genders while working in the mills. Though he became a man, he did not change his tasks, his garments, or his self-presentation at work—he had always been masculine. Which parallels the "enormous struggle within the gay male community to come to terms with the stigma of effeminacy. The most striking result has been a shift from effeminate to masculine styles" (Newton, *Mother Camp*, xiii). An exaggerated masculinity linked, if only rhetorically, to working-class culture, reinforces traditional gender roles, even as it suggests that only one gender is really worth doing.

The gay male steelworkers I interviewed, like the mills in which they work, resist some of the changes that characterize the larger culture. It has gotten harder, rather than easier, for them to be openly gay. The masculinity they embody at work is exaggeratedly traditional—almost a parody of itself, such as that seen in drag performance. Finally, the mill as a space makes possible a category of pleasure, and a category of sex, that has not been possible elsewhere in our culture for many years. The men my narrators had sex with are not gay. The narrators were very adamant about this—in the mill, they insist, having sex with a man does not make you gay. What does, as Jay and others demonstrate, is identifying as gay, and struggling to maintain that identity in a place where it's unwelcome. As Fred observes, having sex with a man in the mill is just being a man who likes sex and gets it wherever and however. Having sex with a *gay* man at work changes everything, by *"making you wonder about yourself,"* which contributes to the severe, repressive secrecy of the men I interviewed.

Studying men in Mississippi in the middle of the twentieth century, John Howard discovers a similar pattern of straight men having sex with gay men. Though many of the gay men felt that their partners must really be gay in some way, in denial or closeted, Howard believes instead that "male-male desire functioned beside and along with many other forms of desire—all at some times, in some places, privileged, oppressed, ignored, overlooked, spoken, silenced, written, thought, frustrated, and acted upon" (123). Unlike people in mid-twentieth-century Mississippi or early twentieth-century New York, people working in steel mills in the twenty-first century are aware of the identity category known as gay, and realize that their behavior might place them within that category. Though I didn't talk to any straight men who say they have sex with other men at work, I conclude from what the gay men I interviewed said that these people feel threatened, and sometimes hostile. The work culture responds by exaggerating masculinity—using gender to counteract sex. The mills were always a "man's world," but when male-male sex presents in that environment—in a cultural climate where male-male sex is considered congruent with homosexuality—hypermasculinity becomes a defense mechanism, a crucial means of identifying as not gay.

This valorization of extreme masculinity affects women as well. Female masculinity attests to this, as does the more intentional, and more humorous, manipulation of gender in drag performance. The bar culture in which many queer steelworkers participate involves plentiful drag performance, in both directions. One man I interviewed had done drag in his youth, though he laughed me off when I asked to see pictures, while another identified as a "dresser," saying he presents as a woman most of the time; and many of the women I interviewed do drag, both informally and competitively. I met some of my narrators in the audience of drag shows, which often motivate local gay folks to get out and be social. The staged performance of drag, and of male impersonation, can tell us something about how queer steelworkers experience and understand the intersections of gender, sexual behavior, class, and tradition.

Much as female steelworkers often feel at home in the mills because that work setting encourages and rewards a masculine, even defensive demeanor that comes naturally to them, drag performance provides a similar "fit." Additionally, male impersonation adds a level of self-conscious humor to the mix. A former student of mine is part of an amateur troupe (which includes at least one steelworker) called Hoosier Daddies. And that's where the parallel with the steel mills comes in: female steelworkers choose their jobs because they enjoy the excitement, the money, and the chance to be themselves. Many wore jackets that advertise their mill affiliation to our interview. They're proud of the work, their ability to do it, and their freedom to act masculine. But perhaps their performance of masculinity is not all that different from that of male steelworkers. To be macho and hypermasculine is also doing "drag"—a performance that steelwork requires of all men, but one that requires extra effort from some gay men. Perhaps that's because, as gay men, staying closeted is a price they pay for being comfortable at work, and in our current social climate, remaining closeted is seen as a sign of weakness—an indicator of a lack of courage or sufficient masculinity. Yet the association of secrecy with "playing it safe" derives from the recurring stereotype that gay people are white, urban, and middle-class. George Chauncey's research on gay New York and Judith Halberstam's thoughts on Brandon Teena, not to mention Kinsey's data, agree with my narrators that being a hidden gay man in an unwelcoming time and/or place makes expanded types of sex and pleasure possible rather than constricting them. According to Halberstam, "the ubiquity of queer sexual practices, for men at least, in rural settings suggests that some other epistemology than the closet governs sexual mores in small towns and wide-open rural areas" (*In a Queer Time and Place* 37). Rather than making queerness impossible, or difficult, the steel mills open up possibilities of pleasure, albeit shameful, secret, and abject. These pleasures circulate around masculinity, and they become harder to indulge openly as the identity-oriented GLBT movement gains momentum, so gender-deviant steelworkers pay a high price for their continuation. Still, the pleasures persist, and thereby suggest the value of a reexamination of what it means to be queer, both in and out of the mill.

CHAPTER SIX

Danger and Death in and out of the Mills

When I ask the steelworkers if their work is dangerous, I always hear that it is, with Hugo summarizing, *"On the tough scale, gay or otherwise, I think this is kind of up there."* This chapter addresses how the day-to-day risk of steelwork, both in terms of accidents and injury on the job, and in terms of long-term health hazards traceable to working in the mill, affects those who do it. Fred points out that you're more likely to be killed on the highway traveling to work than you are on the job, but that doesn't make the work any less deadly. *"I've never seen anyone get seriously hurt. I'm glad. It's happened in my department but I wasn't there. We worked different shifts. I don't know if I'd be able to go back in there if I saw somebody really hurt badly. I've had a couple of really, really close calls—a crane man almost hit me with a slab one day. I've had several crane men carry slabs over my head, and if their crane loses power. . . . The cress haulers, they come and straddle this pile of slabs, and then these tongs come out and they grab the bottom slab and they pick it up high enough that they can get over the other piles of slabs. You could drive easily a pickup truck, maybe a semi underneath there after they have that lifted up, their tires are this wide <indicates a distance of about three feet> and fourteen feet tall, and it was so noisy in there that I jumped down off of my dock in front of this hauler. I heard the stocker shipper go <gasps>, actually he probably shrieked, and I turned around, and the look on the driver's face, I think he probably soiled himself 'cause I was going to be pizza, but I jumped back up on the dock.*

"The mobile equipment, and then the slabs themselves sometimes explode, 'cause of the structure of them. The chemistry of them—they pop open. One of them exploded, there was a gap this wide <he fully extends his arms> I started to fall into, I threw myself, and managed to stay on the slab that had moved over. I mean, I'm standing and suddenly my feet are over here. The stocker had not wrote 'crack sensitive' on there—I was mad. [Here, Fred is referencing a warning label that should be placed on slabs whose production conditions make it more likely that they will explode partly through the burn (cutting) process.] That's part of their job. It's part of my job now to write 'crack sensitive' on there. So the burners know to really watch out. When they get like three

feet to the end, they say stay off of there, 'cause that's when they explode 'cause you've come thirty-six feet down the slab, it's thirty-nine feet long and suddenly BOOM. *It can be really, really dangerous.*

"If I completely erase it out of my mind I'm gonna become a statistic. If I focus on it too much I'll be too paranoid to even go through the gate. Have to be wary but not paranoid. It's hard to learn to do that." This mental adjustment of knowing about the risks but trying to keep that knowledge from paralyzing you is a common strategy among steelworkers.

It's also common for workers to weigh safety against speed. Athena describes the circumstances surrounding the most recent fatality at her mill, and even telling the story seems painful for her. "*The last fatality didn't need to happen. Two mechanics, an old one and a young one in seniority, went down into a pit to change a cylinder. The floor plate that they went under only had a swinging bar to hold it in place. Again, we've done it—it's a nonroutine job, we've done it 150 times over the last 50 years. We've never hit the standing bar with the cylinder before. And that happened. The leg swang out, there was no locking mechanism, and it came down on him. Again we've done this 100 times, and the circumstances just didn't happen, and they happened this time.*

"*A lot of that is educating people. This is what we need to do, this is what we need to look for. If it takes you ten more minutes, or two more hours to do the job, that's what we need to do. Now, management will tell [a worker], 'You've been there a long time. The faster you get it done, the faster you get to go back to the shanty and relax.' So if I tell you to do every safety, and it takes you two hours to set it up, and five minutes to do the job,* OR *you take the risk that you've done a hundred times for the last forty years, are you gonna work for two hours and five minutes, or are you gonna work for five minutes? And that's some of the things you have to change in the mills. If you can move all this material in a fast amount of time, and that's what your father did, your brother did, and you're teaching your kid to do, yeah—that's what makes some of it dangerous. And everything's so big. You've got burning torches, you've got all of those things.*" Free time—to relax with co-workers who feel like family, to eat, to have time alone at least somewhat removed from the overwhelming noise and heat—tempts workers to take shortcuts that might jeopardize their safety.

And then there are hazards that no one can control. Olshana notes cheerfully that she never personally knew anyone who died. "*Mostly the dangers were to do with crushing and maiming. Serious injuries. There was something that would happen in the merchant mills, places where they started out with big pieces of steel and ended up with little rounds. The steel would go through these rolling pins, and the size would get successively smaller, but as it was going through there it would be going faster and faster. There would be a cutting process too. It's called a cobble. If something didn't time out right in this whole process, if it hit an obstruction of some kind, it would start flying through the air, and it would be this molten, red-hot, and if you were in a mill when that happened, there was an alarm, and you would just have to keep your eye on it, because there was no way of knowing where it was going. You'd have this little piece of molten steel bouncing around this room, until it would harden, and then guys would have to go up there and weld it off. That was called a cobble. When that did happen, that was bad, . . . because the smaller it was on the roll lines the faster it would be going."*

I didn't interview any steelworkers over sixty-five because most don't live that long. Many are killed by cancer, heart trouble, accidents, or alcohol before they have been retired more than a few years. Ironically, this means most see little of the relatively high pensions that are one of the putative rewards of this dangerous, stressful work. Happily, I also didn't interview any who were later killed on the job. So my narrators are people who have survived, though their life expectancy is limited. Their stories are packed with accidents, injuries, and cancers, as well as stress, precription and nonprescription drugs, alcohol, and other responses to harsh working conditions. Steelworkers tend to look older than their years due to stress, exhaustion, and the effect of chemicals and heat on human skin. Many of the people I interviewed had intense coughs, vision problems, and nervous mannerisms or expressions that reflected a habitual state of anxiety, worry, and sorrow. It was not unlike visiting a group of war veterans whose histories were carried in every inch of their frames.

But I wonder, as I recall the stories I heard, whether gay people, in all our variety, experience the circumstances of steelwork differently. Lillian Breslow Rubin's account of working-class families notes: "For the men . . . bitterness, alienation, resignation, and boredom are the defining features of the work experience" (159) because the work is repetitive and doesn't reward independent thought. These working conditions increase the odds that workers will be injured, or turn to alcohol. Circumstances such as closeting and harassment add yet another layer of danger and risk to the lives of queer steelworkers. In addition to this type of risk, all steelworkers face dangers both visible and invisible, both immediate and delayed.

Wanda describes three types of dangers to which she is exposed: accidents, silent killers, and gay-bashers. She usually works sitting at a control panel that faces *the moving strip. The strip moves about 2200 square feet per minute. And actually it's in reaching distance. And if there was to be a strip break and the strip was to walk, it could come through. We have safety cages, but it can actually come through, and you can get cut or whatever. If a strip breaks, it's trouble because that strip is jammed up in that machinery. It can fly—I've seen steel fly up in the air 300 feet. Sharp edges. So it's very danger-ous."* Then, she describes the less visible, but equally deadly hazards: *"The atmosphere is not as good. We're running with all different type of chemical solutions, in the mist from the coal. Right now it's wintertime [so] the rolls are cold, and when you put that steel in, that's kinda warm, you're going to get the mist from the oil or whatever solution we're running. The fumes is always gonna be there, particularly on other solutions it's more potent, and you need a fan to like blow it away. But you still breathe it."* These occupational dan-gers compete with people, both in and out of work, who threaten harm to Wanda because she's visibly queer, what she calls *"a stud."*

Though Wanda has been threatened to the point that she fears for her life, the rejection she has faced at home from her brother and, to a lesser extent, her father has made her almost immune to public harassment. She got in a physical fight with her brother, and her father didn't intervene. She came to realize that *"I don't have anybody. I have a sense of feeling alone now in my adult life because I don't feel as if I have the family support that I should have. I put myself in the scenario that if I was on the street arguing with some-one, or if someone was putting their hands on me, I feel as if my father would just drive past. And it hurt me. So bad. This is my brother, this is my blood, for him to call me this stuff and put his hands on me. I expect that from someone in the street. But once I got over the hurt, I felt like I'm glad he did it, because after that point if someone was to make a comment in the streets, it would just blow over my shoulder. It wouldn't affect me as hard."* And people have made comments, and threatened violence, on the street, but that remains much less scary than having it happen at home. It's this nexus of dangerous working conditions, insecure home life, and looming anger and potential antigay violence that make the gay steelworkers lives so challenging. As noted earlier, they usually do not have the support of queer communities who share their experience, unlike most other gay men and women. There are thus few places to turn to make sense of the trade-offs that define their daily lives.

Often, this stress leads to alcoholism. Fred attributes his alcohol abuse specifically to society's hostility toward gay people. He claims that *"25 per-cent of the American population is alcoholic. Amongst gay men, well the figures vary but 80, 85, 90 percent. So 25 percent would have been alcoholic anyway, but because of family pressures, work pressures, internalized homophobia, they use drinking as a coping mechanism, and they become hooked. You don't have to have a family disposition to be an alcoholic. If you drink enough, you become hooked. When you single us out, the alcoholism rates are so much higher. Which is because of how we get treated in this country. It's horrible. Horrible!"* He observes that *"alcoholism has killed almost everybody in my family,"* so it's not limited to queers, it's just that gay people have added reasons to seek out relief from stress, and one of their few outlets is alcohol. The mills have bars just outside the gates that open at 7:00. That's 7:00 A.M.

Many people I interviewed observed that bars have been the only place for GLBT people to meet each other and relax in relative comfort, which contributes to alcohol problems among many queers. Gail, for example, notes that her parents and their parents before them drank as their primary social interaction, but her own situation is even worse, since bars are the only places to which she could turn to find community and potential partners. Zach avoids the local gay bar, wryly noting that *"there seem to be a high number of dependency issues in the gay population."* His partner *"has an alcohol problem,"* and so they avoid the temptation of bars, but it's Zach's understatement that drives his point home.

Jay attributes his problems with alcohol to the stress of working in such a homophobic setting. *"It's a lot of stress. I never planned on things working out this way. A lot of things that happened to me is because of stress. Which is because I'm gay, y'know, trying to find happiness, and I feel lonely, just lonely and vulnerable. And I don't feel like there's enough. I hate that. I feel worse than a black man. I really do. The black people can say that they feel prejudiced against, but they're not. Not as much as we are, 'cause, when they're prejudiced against, there is retribution. If we're prejudiced against, there is no retribution. Even if I get beat up, am I really protected? You know what I'm saying? I think it's just harsh to me. . . . There's so many times I want to say something, I'm a very outspoken person. And I know I can't and I want to and I'm so angry and so mad and sometimes I don't know what I am."* This anger, sense of betrayal, and confusion about identity are responses that the people I interviewed continually expressed when describing the danger of their work. Jay here specifically links his alcoholism to homophobia, to dangerous working conditions, and to lack of cultural support. He longs to be honest about who he is but can't take the risk, and so he feels lost and angry.

Miles agrees that the constant danger of mill work quite literally makes employees mad. *"My grandmother used to be on my grandfather [a steelworker] about drinking, but I guess that's usual because it is a high stress job.*

There's people around that danger day in and day out. They'll be laughing, but it really stinks. It's a high stress job, y'know where you take your life and put it on the line every day. It's also repetitively stressful. You get caught in a situation and you get inundated with all this that you can't usually physically handle and you snap, but you get really intense about it, and angry." Because queer people also face harassment and loneliness, they are even more likely to be angry, self-destructive, or sick.

After working as a summer laborer for four years during college, Hugo took a job for the mill making safety training videos. While a laborer, he had been warned to run if he saw a cobble, or even heard the word, and he had done both, though never as far down as his own work station. The mill he was working in was so hot that everyone had thirty minutes off for every thirty on. To give me a sense of the ever-present danger of the mill, he describes a job he did later. *"I remember doing this safety film in the blast furnace. So I was the camera man, shooting 16-millimeter film, fully decked out in all this safety equipment. The job that we're teaching somebody to do via video is the tapper. So he's the guy who has this great big long pole on the end of which he attaches this thing that looks like a great big long candle, but on the end is an explosive, and there's wires that come out of it. And he's supposed to shove this thing up into this little hole at the bottom of the blast furnace, and then he goes over and connects the wires, and it blows up, and steel, molten steel comes out. So the supervisor says, 'I'm going to put my hand on your shoulder. If there's a problem with the blast, I'm going to pull you back, and then I want you to run.' I mean, I'm there for three hours. This is what they do. So you know, on the tough scale, gay or otherwise, I think this is kind of up there. This is kind of dangerous. It's almost like a military job. Anything could happen. But those were the kind of jobs people were doing."*

Bernard witnessed an explosion at a basic oxygen furnace (4BOF) where he worked, and in the months following this incident experienced stress at home and harassment on the job (a pretty constant thing for him). This combination got to be too much for him, and he was diagnosed with Post-Traumatic Stress Disorder. He describes the incidents that led to his diagnosis, for which he went untreated. *"Two men were killed at the 4BOF for cutting into a 25,000-pound oxygen line, . . . where it blew up, and they were dismembered. I will never forget that day. It was early in the morning around 8, 9 o'clock. There was an explosion, and . . . I'm the closest so I go up to the sixth floor, I see the section manager . . . walking towards the north direction along a narrow catwalk on the sixth floor. I look to my right 'cause I'm at the south end of the stairwell near the blast explosion. First it was clear, then I get*

Cold steel scrap charge headed toward opened electric furnace, Inland Steel,
East Chicago, ca. 1970. Courtesy of the Calumet Regional Archives.

*a vague impression of something blue on the other side of the junction point,
which is like at a forty-five-degree angle. Then when I got towards it, to see that
there was a person standing there, a blast of steam covered my path, where I
couldn't see, so I held onto the railing, so I could see where I was going, and as
I made it slowly through a cloud, there was a man in a odd-looking suit. . . .
All I could see was his face, the outline of his shoulders. His hands I could not
see because [the] only portions I could see was from his waist up. There was an
outline but I couldn't see no definition. . . . I could tell that he was white, he had
blue eyes, but the one thing that stood out to me, other than the suit, he had
the arc of a camera flash in his eyes. And it was strange. I remember going by
him and I remember seeing a splatter of blood and a shoe and part of a charred
bone sticking out and at some point I must have panicked or something because I remember running back, and at some point I must have flipped over
something because I went down six flights of stairs. . . . My back still bothers me
to this day. After the explosion . . . I started having emotional problems. . . . And
I started having problems at work where either consciously or unconsciously I
would hurt myself. And I started having problems with sleep. I was diagnosed
for traumatic stress disorder. But I didn't get nothing for it. Those guys that got
exploded? Those white guys that knew the guys, they gave them two weeks off
with pay. Nobody, the man told me I'd be all right, to drive myself home. And
I did, and I was back to work the following Monday."* The incredible level of

detail in Bernard's story gives a sense of the emotional and mental impact that witnessing this event had on him. He can't forget what he saw, and by his own account, this experience made him nervous, prone to accidents, and ill.

Two narrators who work for their mills' emergency services division had abundant stories of death and destruction. Renee summarizes the dangers of steelwork this way: *"Any part of the mill can be dangerous, I mean you've got molten iron, flowing, in places and that just shouldn't be, y'know, when you think about it. There's heavy machinery, I mean, we have accidents from the big huge machines. You'd have to see them to get a sense—the tires are about as big as this wall here, um, y'know types of ukes [a brand of giant dump truck] that run into a pickup truck, and when something like that runs into a pickup truck, it's not good. Or in the shops, y'know, all types of heavy equipment with pinch points, and somebody goes to move something and accidentally gets their glove caught or whatever and now they're stuck in that machinery. It's dangerous, kind of, anywhere you go, really. And when things are on fire and exploding and all of that, we're the ones that are going in there when everyone's getting out. So over the years, ladles break out, I mean you get a crack in 'em, and you got molten iron on the ground. That's typical. I mean, you cool it off and keep it from running, to where y'know you've got things that are actually exploding. You've got molten iron and water, and it just doesn't mix and it explodes. So, y'know, there's plenty of fires out there."* Some rescues she finds painful to describe, which I conclude based on her reluctance to talk about them in any detail and her visible difficulty getting the words out, yet overall she gives a sense of loving the excitement and of feeling important and valued.

Yesenia, another EMS fire service worker, captures this paradox well. She describes several heartbreaking fatalities, ending with this one: *"We've had um, gosh, two railcars workin' side by side, the switchmen went between the two switches, between the two rails to do a switch, between the cars, and when he went to do it somebody remotely operated this one and it pinned him between the two and then when you have that much pressure pinned, naturally your organs get smashed. The minute you release it you're gonna bleed out. So we contacted his family and said 'You need to come see him.' So we cover him up, family comes, they were talkin', they did their goodbyes, the family leaves, [we] disconnect the railcars, he dies. Yeah, so, it's gory sometimes, but sometimes it's kind of cool. You'll get that guy that has a heart attack and falls out and then he comes back and he tells you about it."* Yesenia gets satisfaction from the work—it is fast-paced, varied, and feels important. Though anything this dramatic is also going to be stressful, supportive co-workers and a sense of connection to the work community (which, as noted earlier, are more likely to be experienced in the mills by lesbians than by gay men) act to mitigate that for her.

Queer people are at higher risk for developing cancer than the general population. There are several possible reasons for this. First, 36 percent of GLBT people smoke, while only 25 percent of all adults do (gay.com). Second, gay people face stress from being a stigmatized population, and stress may lead to increased cancer rates. Third, diagnosis or treatment of cancer can be delayed by the fact that many queers have uneasy relationships with the medical establishment. Generally, doctors try to treat all patients alike, without noticing that this means treating all patients as if they were straight. They don't usually ask what gender your sexual partners are, who constitutes your support system, or what unusual stressors society may have aimed at you. The National LGBT Cancer Network works to train doctors in dealing with queer patients, because, as the group's website explains, "previous or feared negative responses from health care providers frequently keep too many LGBT individuals from seeking routine care and cancer screening . . . suggesting that inaccessible health care together with the preponderance of discrimination and homophobia in the health care system contribute to decreased screening rates, putting LGBT individuals at a greater risk of late stage cancer diagnosis ("Barriers to Health Care"). This delay can make treatment less rapid and less successful. Finally, gay people tend to be more "out" about their cancer status (though my narrators don't fit this pattern). Revealing that you have cancer is an awkward personal disclosure that frequently makes listeners uncomfortable. Since cancer is usually not visible, many people choose not to reveal their illness, wanting to avoid hostility or unproductive concern. My narrators in particular usually waited to be asked about it, which corresponds with their habits of guarded disclosure and secrecy.

Many of the people I interviewed had cancer, usually lung cancer or mesothelioma. Gail has lymphoma. One of the jobs she performed was monitoring the troughs of molten iron. The ladle pours the liquid metal down troughs, from which it runs into molds. Gail's job was to watch closely for any hardening (which could plug up the trough, causing an overflow) and administer coke breeze to troubling spots. She describes *"sprinkling"* the coke breeze, whose consistency and sparkle reminded her of *"fairy dust."* She doesn't attribute her cancer to this particular job, but I do.

Victor has asthma and regular lung inspections following being *"dusted"* at work. *"There were about forty-six different types of carcinogens that I inhaled real bad. I'm still on medication. From two years ago about this time. I was hauling dust from a blast furnace—it's coke and iron and magnesium, zinc, copper, everything that goes into this, and they dump it into our truck, and they're supposed to put water on it, and because it's wintertime they don't do it, and they do it at night so the EPA can't see, and it goes up in the air; well they loaded me up, and I couldn't see nothing—I couldn't even see the semi. So we let the dust settle, and I was loaded, and had to go out and you got—it's a real narrow road we got to go out—you got to watch so your mirrors don't get knocked off—you're right underneath the blast furnace. And I pulled off because I couldn't see out my windows, so I got out to wipe my windows off. Well, they dumped another load on the truck behind me, and the air come down on me, and I inhaled all this stuff and I couldn't breathe, and I'm over on the other side of the truck, so I try to get in, but I couldn't get in—the door was locked, so I'm trying to get back over to the driver's side to get into the truck, and I'm inhaling all this stuff. By the time I got on the radio, my mouth is just full of it, my lungs are full of it, my nostrils just full of it. Since then I've been on an inhaler and a nasal spray for two years, since this happened."* Victor says that company medical says he shouldn't have left his truck, or should have worn a mask, and that he'll be fine. I'm skeptical.

Neither of these incidents relates to being gay—they're just part of life in this work setting. Blue-collar and industrial workers have a higher incidence of cancer than the general population, just as queer people do, and my narrators fall into *both* high risk-groups. They live, or more often die, dangerously.

The extent to which you take care of your body is directly related to how much you value it, and yourself. More than half of my narrators had been molested as children—and the total could be higher since I'm including only the people who chose to tell me about it—a proportion well above that for the general population. Does surviving childhood sexual abuse give you cancer or alcohol addiction, or steer you toward challenging, dangerous jobs? Not directly, no. But maybe it encourages you to believe that you are valueless, and that your preferences and comfort can be disregarded.

Most of my narrators knew the abuse they reported was wrong and that the adult was an evil predator, but they often felt guilt as well and confusion about the episode's connection to their future sexual preference. Nate describes this dilemma: *"I've always been attracted to older men. And I think part of that is when I was very, very young I was raped by an older man,*

Locomotive pulling Pugh ladle cars (transporting molten metal from the blast furnace
to the open-hearth furnaces or BOFs), Inland Steel, East Chicago, ca. 1980.
Courtesy of the Calumet Regional Archives.

repeatedly, over a period of time. But I got the affirmation from that man that I
never felt I got from my father. With my father I could spit gold coins and it was
never quite good enough. Platinum would have been better. This gentleman,
even though it was not something that I was wanting to do, and it was not
something comfortable for me, affirmed the fact that I was good. And so older
men became a fascination for me." Few of the women I interviewed disclosed
a history of childhood sexual abuse, which surprised me both because we
know that its incidence among all women is very high and because many
did discuss sexual violence they had experienced, or fended off, as adults.
My guess is that, though some probably had experienced sexual abuse
as girls, the stories they told themselves, and thus me, emphasized their
toughness and control—they tried to embody a masculine story of triumph
by choosing what stories to remember and then pass on.

Most of the victims I spoke to feel responsible because they did not stop
the rapes, which, in many cases, continued for years. Instead, they frequently believe that being raped shaped their sexual preference, or that
the perpetrators were drawn to them because they seemed willing or interested. Fred tells me that *"I believe sexual molestation—men attack small boys*
because they're gay—they're already gay, that's what makes the men attracted

to them. That's just an opinion. A lot of gay men talk about being molested as children." And Jay reports that a guy across the street *"propositioned me in an abandoned house and had sex. I was fifteen years old going on sixteen, and I didn't stop it, you know what I mean? I should have, but I didn't, because I was afraid. I didn't want my father to know because this guy threatened me, and told me he would tell. I didn't know what I was thinking. But it happened."* In these and other stories, the men take some responsibility for what happened, and seek to understand what impact this experience has had on their adult sexuality and their work life.

Childhood sexual abuse is only the most dramatic form of the lifelong pattern of bigotry, harassment, and violence that GLBT steelworkers face. By the time most find work in the mills, they are, to some extent, trained in dealing with a hostile, dangerous world. Mary Lindenstein Walshok argues, in her study *Blue-Collar Women*, that lesbians persist even in unpleasant and dangerous jobs because they're already used to being marginalized and have ample "practice living as an outsider" (109). Danielle agrees with this assessment, noting offhandedly that the harassment and risk she feels in the mill is no different from the *"double-takes and stares"* (not to mention hostile comments, violence, and rape) that have been a part of her life for as long as she can remember. Those who can adjust to this "atmosphere of constant harassment" and thus keep their mill jobs are people who "have certain qualities as survivors, one of which is the ability to accommodate brusque male behavior" (Olson 107). Queers, and lesbians in particular, are better equipped for steel jobs because they are probably already used to such treatment, and thus able to respond to it offensively, rather than feel demoralized and hurt.

Fred links the abuse and gay-bashing that many queers experience to anger and alcohol in later life. *"Drag queens are some of the meanest people you'll ever meet. Cause of all the treatment we get. It just pisses you off. I had never had a mean streak until I got beaten up. It raised up something really ugly. I really don't recommend it. Don't fuck with me—you might be taking your life in your hands. Not a good idea. And I'm much nicer than most people—and most gay people. Lot of 'em are just mean, bitter, hurt people. They grew up being abused."* As Fred's story suggests, a lifetime of harassment and abuse can lead to violence and anger, as well as make surviving and thriving in a difficult work setting possible.

The female steelworker most explicit about her anger was Carmen. Finally retired and beginning a new life in college, Carmen resents that she gave her life to the mill and got nothing in return. *"I was burned over 60 percent of my body in an accidental spill, and it took years of skin grafts and rehab for me to be able to move again—for me to get my life back."* She has ongoing health problems, lost a baby, and says she never felt fairly treated by the company or the union because of her race, her gender, *and* her sexuality. She is reluctant to describe these experiences because she wants to move away from the anger and frustration, to lead a life that is more positive.

Anger was a recurring theme, especially for the men I interviewed. It would be interesting to know whether all steelworkers (or maybe all male steelworkers) discuss anger this much, or whether queers feel and express more anger. Ben protests that he is *not* angry, though *"I was a very angry person when I was younger. I'm now very calm. Yes, I may get angry enough so that we may cross words, but give me a few minutes to calm down and I'll apologize for yelling at you, 'cause that means I lost my temper. I control my anger a lot more than you'd think."* The steelworkers often link anger with self-control, with masculinity, and with firearms, though usually in fun. Jay told me, *"I am stubborn, I am impatient. I'm not impatient to the point where I would want to kill somebody. I think cars should have Uzis in the front of them, but that's me."* Though there's clearly some anger underneath this teasing, Jay goes on to note that the real anger, the scary anger isn't in gay people, but toward them. Then he says, *"I'm not living a lie, everyone else is."* Anger is where this chapter's two threads—the danger of steelwork and the danger of queerness—intersect. Being gay is dangerous not because gay people are angry, but because other people, presumably straight, are hostile and violent toward us.

Fear of angry straight people is what keeps so many queer steelworkers closeted. Since teamwork is so crucial in the mills, and your life can frequently depend on a co-worker's intervening quickly to help you, gay people often decide not to take the risk of disclosure. Athena is brutally frank about this thought process. *"You have to rely on your co-workers in the steel mill. You not only have to rely on you—you have to rely on them. And in the back of your mind, are you thinking, if something happens, are they gonna turn their back? 'Cause they kinda wish you were dead anyway?"* Keeping the secret, and worrying about somehow "slipping" are both very stressful, as is the fear that if you do tell, your life might be the price you pay.

Shift work, sometimes called swing shift, also causes stress and illness. Erin worked in the slab yard, doing physical work in extreme temperatures, but she says the hardest part *"was adjusting your life to a schedule which changed on a constant basis. A lot of the people in the mill have jobs where you don't know 'til Thursday what you're going to be working the following week."*

Roll stands at the 80" hot strip, ArcelorMittal Steel, East Chicago, 2011.
Photograph by the author.

This schedule makes arranging for day care nearly impossible, and anything involving a schedule challenging. And years of irregular sleep is very hard on the body. Phil lists shift work as the most dangerous aspect of his job, noting that *"They've been watching a study on sleep shift disorders, but as of right now they haven't decided that's really a disorder yet."* Mills don't want to change this system, in spite of its cost to the workers. I often asked why each worker wasn't assigned a permanent shift and was told that this would be unfair and hazardous. If any given shift has a shortage of experienced workers, disaster might result. With assigned shifts, senior workers would be slotted into better shifts, leaving less-experienced workers clustered in undesirable ones.

Though management's justification of this schedule makes some sense, shift work is ultimately exhausting and dehumanizing. Having no control over your schedule, and thus minimal control over your social and family life, inclines workers to feel alienated and valueless. Renee observes that *"in steel mills, y'know, a lot of people feel like numbers. They can replace you, there will be somebody right behind you trying to get in, and you get people in there that, I mean, it's a good job, it's a good paying job, but the sacrifices that some people make being in the steel mill. I mean you look at some of these people who are now retiring and they've been there forty years, and they've devoted their life to that job, and their kids have grown up and they haven't been there. And a lot of them still to this day work swing shift, and I've been working swing shift for ten years, and every week it's a different shift, and every day you go into work you don't know if you're there for eight hours, for twelve hours, for sixteen hours, if somebody calls off, somebody's got to fill that turn. So you kind of give up some things to have the money. Swing shift is horrible. Your body doesn't get acclimated. Every week it changes. Now they're coming out with shift work disorders and all this other stuff. I don't have children, so the most I have to worry about is my dog, getting the neighbor to let him out and that, but y'know it's hard, and the other thing is you might not have weekends off. You might be there fifteen, twenty years before you have weekends off. . . . I guess work becomes your life, and you schedule things around work, it's not like you have your weekends free, and that, sometimes you might work for years and have days during the week off and everybody, your friends, has weekends off."*

This schedule causes exhaustion, illness, and a lack of social routine. Zach's mill rotates between two twelve-hour shifts, because layoffs led them to eliminate one of the previous eight-hour shifts, yet they still needed to keep the plant constantly running. So he switches between working 7:00 A.M. to 7:00 P.M. and working 7:00 P.M. to 7:00 A.M. If you add in commuting and sleep time, there is almost no time left for social interaction, which is especially important for queer steelworkers, who are isolated at work and often can't share their lives much there, so need social time to connect with a supportive community. Though many people I interviewed do think of their co-workers as family, they often want to carve out time to be with other gay people, making the swing shift schedule another of the extra challenges faced by GLBT steelworkers.

CHAPTER SEVEN

Unions in Twenty-First-Century America

Unions, the labor movement, and the United Steelworkers of America are a recurring topic in the steelworkers' stories, and so have already been mentioned in earlier chapters, but I want to deal with them in more detail here, and with some of the problems surrounding them. As a progressive with working-class roots, I believe in unions and what they stand for. I know what unions have made possible for all American workers, and I respect the hard work and sacrifice that lie behind the changes unions have achieved. And some steelworkers I interviewed share this view, but many don't. When a union-busting right-to-work law was passed by the Indiana legislature in February 2012, I was crushed and angry. The next day, I heard from one of my narrators, who supported the new law, claiming that it might finally make the unions fight for the allegiance of their workers rather than continue to line their own pockets and keep people in highly paid jobs that they no longer really perform. Can I tell him he's wrong, when each morning he crosses the tracks to make steel, while I sit in my office writing?

In general, the steelworkers I spoke to are unenthusiastic about their union. Most are members of the USW, but some are Longshoremen (the union that serves all of the Port of Indiana) and others, such as Heavy Equipment Operators, belong to separate unions that contract workers out to the steel mills. I did my interviews between 2009 and 2012, when unions had been under so much pressure for so long that they had to choose their battles carefully in order to win any protection for their workers. To these political realities imposed from outside, add years of real or perceived corruption and infighting within the unions, and you get a sense of why support is eroding from within the rank and file.

The USW has a specific history in the United States that makes many steelworkers feel alienated from it. Late in the nineteenth century, steel and mine workers joined together and formed a new union called the Amalgamated, which organized (and lost) a big strike in 1919. Following this debacle, they lost power. When the first big national union (the American Federation of Labor, or AFL) emerged, it was largely a craft union organization, with trades such as electricians, millwrights, and carpenters each looking out for its own interests. As Mike Olszanski (a longtime steelworker, union activist, and now labor studies instructor) says, John L. Lewis noticed that this strategy left unskilled and semi-skilled workers unorganized. As industry in the United States grew, with many workers being unskilled, Lewis saw his chance, and founded the Congress of Industrial Organizations, or CIO (ultimately, the AFL and CIO joined forces, but they began as competing national groups of unionized workers). Lewis was then pivotal in creating the SWOC (Steel Workers Organizing Committee), which organized large steel mills across all skilled and unskilled jobs, and which ultimately became the USWA in 1942. Since Lewis had years of experience in unions already, he (and his right-hand man, Philip Murray, the first president of the USWA and the CIO) knew how to write union rules and regulations so that Lewis maintained control rather than being susceptible to unrest from the rank and file. There was some early communist involvement in the USWA and other American unions, but in the mid to late 1940s, the Red Scare changed that (personal interview, November 5, 2012).

Mike Olszanski (who worked maintenance in the mills starting in 1966) observes that a Cold War mentality had a widespread and long-standing effect on the USWA. No one wanted to appear communist, and since unions are structured around collective action, fear of "red taint" was especially strong among them. Olszanski (nicknamed "Oz") told me that every member of the rank and file, and especially people active in union organizing, lived in fear of being accused of being pink. This fear decreased unions' effectiveness, since collective bargaining and strikes were risky by definition. Any local (such as the leftist-run 1010 at Inland Steel where Oz worked) that was militant or strove aggressively to fight the "restructuring" of steelworkers that led to huge job losses in the 1980s could be discredited and stripped of power through a mere accusation of communist tendencies. This general crippling of unions, combined with the top-down structure of the USW, clarifies why steelworkers feel frustrated with their union, even though many still support it and work within it to make change.

Beyond the general dissatisfaction many workers feel, gay workers are likely to experience additional alienation from organized labor. Their specific concerns are not likely to receive prominence in a climate where unions fight to maintain any unified, coherent negotiating position. Many of my narrators are extremely hostile and bitter toward their union because they feel it has not helped keep them safe or sane. Though I may not share their negative assessment of the union or feel as skeptical as they of the

USW's ability to help them forge a more supportive, safer working environment, it is clear that many of them are disgruntled.

While balancing my feelings against theirs, I also face a philosophical problem inherent in oral history research. Post-Enlightenment humans feel irresistibly compelled to value the individual—to believe that each person is master of his or her own destiny and that creating change is the responsibility of each of us. We tend to think that if something is wrong with someone's situation, or a person is unhappy, then that person should take action and find a solution. Though we know that this is partly a fantasy—that larger forces are at work against which we as individuals are helpless—it's still a very powerful myth, whose attractiveness should be kept in mind, even as we try to resist it.

Oral history reinforces this myth by collecting life stories of individuals who are, by the very nature of the interview process, seen as principle actors in the drama of their own lives. The assumption is that people have agency, and that our actions matter. However, post-structuralism and queer theory argue that human subjects—our actions, our desires, and our interpretations—are always already shaped by language, culture, history, context.

Ronald J. Grele sets the parameters of the field of oral history in *Envelopes of Sound*, which he co-wrote with Studs Terkel and others. He cautions that because oral historians ask people to reflect on their lives, narrators often notice things they had never really noticed before. Oral historians are supposed to ask questions that get narrators to think about their lives, which can make them become conscious of mundane details that had not seemed worth remembering before (253). One problem with this method, especially in the United States, where the rhetoric of individualism prevails, is that the focus on a narrator alone isolates him or her from communities and institutions, suggesting that "individuals shape their own destinies, that they are in some way historical actors, and this by choice" (256). Unions, by contrast, are about collective action. They remind us that we do not act alone, and that John Henry died. Though the image of the individual student halting the tanks in Tiananmen Square (during a protest in 1989) is powerful and memorable, we know that he and many other protestors were dead within days.

As an oral historian, I find the steelworkers' stories of victimization and resistance compelling and moving. When their unions don't back them up, I feel disappointed and angry. Yet at the same time, I know that any union's first priority is to protect the jobs, lives, and salaries of as many workers as possible. Both rhetorically and politically, both individual and collective modes can coexist. It's a matter of "both/and" rather than "either/or" when it comes to oral histories' culpability in hegemonic discourse and as a source of individual *and* collective change. Furthermore, I believe that the USW can do a better job of protecting the steelworkers I interviewed, and the many others whose stories are still untold, than it is doing now. Workers' right to express their sexual orientation and gender identity need to be protected in their contract. More important, there needs to be a change of culture in the mills. All workers need to acknowledge that queers are everywhere, that we work in all jobs even when we are not visible and choose not to make ourselves visible, and that the work climate of everybody will improve when *all* workers are respected. But before this utopia arrives, we need to honestly examine the experience gay steelworkers of all kinds have within their unions and the attitudes that scholars and others have about unions and queers and their interrelationship.

In a 2007 volume called *The Sex of Class*, an essay by Gerald Hunt and Monica Bielski Boris, "The Lesbian, Gay, Bisexual, and Transgender Challenge to American Labor," presents a historical overview of unions' changing interest in LGBT issues. It concludes that the more white-collar a union is, and the more female members it has, the more likely it is to be open to queer issues. The best example of this is the SEIU (Service Employees International Union) whose president, Mary Kay Henry, is an open lesbian. "In addition, all the less responsive and unresponsive unions are private-sector unions representing a blue-collar, largely male work force" (93). This group, of course, describes the steelworkers. Research by Embrick, Walther, and Wickens argues that unions' "attitudes and behaviors sustain rigid boundaries around masculinity and are frequently utilized to create a white working-class male solidarity based on the perseverance of heteronormativity" (765). By this analysis, queer steelworkers are not only invisible to their own unions, but also stigmatized as a means for unions to gain a sense of unity and coherence under pressure. Intense labor competition, of the sort we see today, also creates fear and uncertainty among workers, which can easily translate into prejudice.

Several people I interviewed went to work in the mills as part of a leftist political agenda. They wanted to become industrial workers in order to help bring about a revolution from within the rank and file. Janis is one such person, and she claims that the USW's lack of support for queers has a long history. She notes that old-school communists believed that gay people were an especially degenerate part of the bourgeoisie, producing no children and creating a market for frivolous items such as smoking jackets. Janis claims that many of the initial organizers of the USW, back when it was mainly a coal mining organization, were communists trained in Russia, who subscribed to these beliefs. Her history is sometimes inaccurate (for example, John L. Lewis hired 200 party members, none of whom had been trained in the Soviet Union), yet a resistance to gay people and our issues still prevailed among steelworkers, and Janis provides a story that attributes a historical origin to these feelings of oppression. She claims, *"We can't understand any of this unless we understand where each union originated. The steel unions came from the coal mining unions, which were organized by communists. Early in the twentieth century, leftist leaders who wanted to unionize the miners brought over a few well-trained organizers from Eastern Bloc communist countries. These Soviets worked to form those unions, in the South, which were integrated right from the start. When I worked at Inland, the union was perfectly integrated, one-third blacks, one-third Hispanics, and one-third whites. But this angered the Klan. I worked with a guy who remembered, as a kid, his dad and uncle were steelworkers in the union, and when the Klan came to the house, they'd make the kids get under the bed and the men would stand at the window with guns, and shoot till the Klan left.*

"Joseph Stalin hated the homosexuals. He said they were products of capitalism. You wonder where he thought the Greeks came from? Capitalism took off in the twentieth century, while we queers have been here all along. But that's one of the things that made unions, and working-class people influenced by them, hate homosexuals. And work to exclude them. At least at the beginning. Then during the 40s and 50s, when McCarthyism came in and they did the red-baiting, the unions all went mainstream and denied any connection to communism. They had to . . . So parts of Communism didn't really make sense, but that's where the Unions we have now come from. And that effects how they act."

During the period Janis is describing (early 1900s) no political or cultural theorists had a progay agenda, so her blaming early communists for her sense that today's unions don't attend to the needs of queers is somewhat arbitrary. Yet she constructs a historical story—an origin myth—to help her understand the unequal treatment she has experienced. The accuracy of the myth is less important than her need to explain why her union, which she loves, systematically neglects her, simultaneously citing and coercing her invisibility.

Union leaders assert that gay steelworkers often avoid filing harassment complaints because they believe that the union does not support them, and thus it's difficult for the organization to protect them. Many steelworkers agree with this analysis, pointing out that filing a complaint is tantamount to painting a target on themselves. Some workers said that they have filed complaints, and know of co-workers who have done so as well, but these complaints seem never to make it past the first step of the grievance procedure. Andy, for example, notes: *"I know for a fact that guys have filed stuff or at least went to their foreman about it, and foremen haven't done anything about it. I mean, and . . . the union just kinda smoothes it over with the person, tries to tell them you know, they didn't mean it that way, let's not get anybody fired here, that kind of stuff. It's like, you know, they kind of turn a blind eye to it, you know what I mean, it's something that they don't want to have to deal with."*

Since the 1980s downsizing, the unions are in such a weak position that they tend to avoid any controversy they perceive as "divisive." The steel unions lost most of their power at about the same time queers began to be visible enough to need and seek protection, and queer steelworkers agree that the unions did not take the risk of defending their vulnerable populations. Chris, though not explicitly out at work, was frequently harassed for perceived gay behavior. To pass for straight, all men learn to exaggerate certain masculine traits and distance themselves from anything associated with femininity. This means that you can be perceived as gay if your posture, diction, inflection, or attitude are insufficiently predatory and "macho." Chris observes that the union officially prevents the workplace harassment he experienced, but that it relies on the workers to document what is happening, and often doesn't push cases through. He remembers, *"I had a couple punks, someone said something to somebody and this guy's giving me a hard time, so I talked to the person who was in charge of that at the [union] hall, and when she talked to this punk, he was a little punk who needed his ass kicked, a little twerp, and I'm not a violent person. I'm not one to scream or jump up and down. But, really nothing came of it. Then another guy, in this same area started to pull the same setup, and I really just felt, what's the use. And my griever says, 'well, just stay away from that area.' Well, that's part of my area that I've got to work in. The mill's a half a mile long, and a half of it I cover, and sometimes I need to go through that area, or some other area and sometimes I have to deal with him directly because he works on some of the same things I do, so we have to work with each other.*

"But one of the bigger problems I've had is, you've got these macho, macho Mexican guys that were raised with this garbage, and they think that I'm the one that should be ignored. One kid was saying that I was saying things to him, and

I was like, 'sorry, honey, you ain't my type.' But that's a curious thing out there. It's nice to think you have the union backing, but sometimes you don't . . . 'cause I've had a couple times where I've had to deal with the hall, and they weren't a whole lotta help." When even an educated, politicized steelworker like Chris, who knows his rights and is willing to fight for them, says he can't get his union representative to defend him, I have to conclude that queer steelworkers often feel defenseless and vulnerable at work.

Keith, a much younger steelworker just out of high school, doesn't even believe that the union is *supposed* to protect him. He observes that most gay steelworkers don't frequent gay bars, even in Chicago, because they *"are pretty scared. Nobody wants to be recognized. I really don't care. I'm not going to broadcast it, but. . . . You do know that equal opportunity—sexual orientation—isn't always a protected right? Like in our contract it's not. Um, if they find out I'm gay and they find a reason to fire me, I can't sue them because they fired me for being gay. In my contract it's only race, religion, sex, and age. The Union makes these standards."* According to Keith, then, the union not only doesn't encourage harassed gay workers to file complaints, it also sets policy that doesn't consider them a protected group. Whether this is true of his union or not, Keith believes it, so he stays closeted at work.

And Keith is not alone—Phil describes constant antigay banter among his co-workers. *"There are days now where I get so fed up with the gay jokes— people are gay, this is gay, things like that, for example, when Ricky Martin came out, people were like, someone must have molested him when he was a child for him to become gay. And it just took everything I had—that was right when I first accepted this, so. I don't feel right now that I'm strong enough to take that fight on by myself."* This conversation is hard for Phil; my guess is that being caught between being true to himself and true to his work milieu is stressful for him. He blames this difficult trap on explicit union policy, noting, *"Even if you look at our union's equal opportunity policy, it doesn't even mention sexual orientation—it's that race, creed, color, sex thing."*

The tradeswomen that Jane LaTour chronicles in her account *Sisters in the Brotherhoods* often faced problems such as these from their unions. What sets LaTour apart from other scholars of women in nontraditional jobs is that she discusses lesbians explicitly and extensively, while so many other scholars tacitly assume that all women are straight or that sexuality does not matter. The lesbians she interviewed got minimal support from their unions (not the USWA, just to be clear). On the contrary, LaTour tells how one carpenter used the union to get the promotion she deserved but was then left to navigate a very hostile workplace where, as she says, "I feel like I often get the short end of the stick, the tools and the resources available there. I'm just not a full-fledged team player. I feel like I have less information than everybody else, like I'm working blind a lot" (119). Pornography permeated her workplace, and she used union channels to reduce it, and again "I won the battle but lost the war. . . . The hostility towards me was what eventually led to my demise. . . . I can't believe the hatred that ensued from wanting the dirty pictures down. On the surface it improved, but it manifested itself in other ways, with pockets of hatred and sabotage directed at me throughout my tenure there, which, I believe, ultimately led to my demise" (120). Thus, even when her union intervened to help her, it did not address the underlying problems that led to the harassment, and she paid a high price for even that much support.

When sexuality isn't an issue, the union is often very helpful. Miles worked as a shop steward and as a griever, and prides himself on getting most of the grievances he wrote past the first step of the hearing process. And Olshana got help from the union when she was given an unfair test. She explains that *"when it was time for me to take my final test to be a motor inspector, it was a hands-on test, and they gave me an instrument to use that I had never been trained on. So, I didn't pass the test. So I filed a grievance. And the union helped me win that—I hadn't been trained on that piece of equipment so it wasn't fair that I be tested on it. So they agreed that I should be trained on that piece of equipment, and then tested again. Which is what happened, and I passed. I had to file a grievance, but it was useful, and they were good."* Though Olshana reports that *"once I went into the shanty or onto the floor, I can't remember ever working with, around, or near a woman—it was really a man's world,"* she felt that the union supported her when she demonstrated her case. Olshana was not out at work, and she never asked for union support around issues of harassment, which may have contributed to a more positive experience for her.

In general, the union will process what it considers to be a "legitimate" complaint against the company but will use its influence to downplay internal problems. Outsiders may assume that union members and working-class people in general see the value of unions, which face opposition chiefly from management. But that assumption is not born out by the steelworkers I interviewed, most of whom were at least guardedly critical of their union. Paul Clemens, who haunted a closing auto plant for a year, getting to know the workers, found similar dissatisfaction. He summarizes, "Detroit is a union town, but anti-union feeling . . . is not uncommon" (111). One person working for a small contractor says his boss is "working on a program to get

Moving coils, 80" hot strip, Inland Steel, East Chicago, 1985.
Courtesy of the Calumet Regional Archives.

us retirement benefits, insurance. But we're not union, and he won't have a driver that is union. Never happen. He'll tell you that a union will break a company in a heartbeat" (206). Another observes, "I want nothing to do with a union, . . . I don't want somebody regulating my life. My family relies on my paycheck entirely too much" (213). This last worker claims that unions regulate jobs excessively, so that they take longer and cost more. For him, there's a trade-off between regulation and efficiency. As these comments show, many workers at the start of the twenty-first century do not endorse or defend unions.

One reason unions have lost power in recent decades is that newer and younger workers do not know labor history and tend to valorize individualism and meritocracy. These workers, especially in a declining industry in times of recession, are willing to take almost any job, and are not well educated about the unions. As Renee puts it, the mills are *"hiring a bunch of younger workers—kids—early twenties. They have no idea what a union is. They have no idea what it's supposed to do, how it works. Nothing. They're out for themselves. They want money. They will work whatever hours you ask of them because they don't have families, they want the money. They don't care. I had a kid that I was training the other day ask me: 'Why do we have the union?' I said, do you understand that you have the wages, you're getting paid what you're making because of the union, because they fought over the years to get you the wages that you are making? Do you realize that without a union they could fire you tomorrow and it doesn't matter? Just because they want to. I said, you really need to go on the computer when you have some time and sit down and do a little research on unions. But that's what they want to hire. That's who they want to get in there—young and dumb. And ones they can manipulate and they can promise the world to, and you're going to move up, and you're going to do this, and you're going to do that. And that's consistently what they've done over the last few years is hire these young kids. And the ones that are older, they are trying to make them walk towards the door."* Renee believes that she and her former partner, also a mill worker, have been repeatedly passed over for promotion, not only because they are gay women, but also because they know their rights and use the union to defend them. She summarizes: *"They don't like women who are outspoken. That's definitely going to get you nowhere."*

Queers in the mills, then, are in a damned-if-you-do, damned-if-you-don't situation regarding unions. If you turn to the union for backing, as Renee and her former partner did, management may retaliate, denying you future promotions or advantages. But if you resist going to the union, usually out of the belief that it wouldn't help much anyway, you either continue to get bullied and miss out on the promotion, or remain in the closet to prevent it and miss out on the promotion as well. Tommy was constantly verbally harassed at work and was beaten to the point of hospitalization when leaving a local bar. But he reflects, *"I never really confronted the union. I thought about doing it at one time, but they hadn't really done anything drastic, it was just bullying. But we're grown men, y'know? Even though I was only in my 20s and early 30s, but I knew the union was not going to do anything. I doubt that anyone goes there, 'cause they don't want anyone else to know, with the fear that the union won't support 'em, y'know?"* An even stronger position is well articulated by Xena: *"I'll tell you about the unions. Unions suck. They creep up on you and side with the company."* And Bernard notes repeatedly, and with increasing bitterness, *"The union doesn't do anything"* since *"they're looking out for the company's interest, they're not looking out for you."*

In the past thirty years unions have made many concessions in an effort to keep jobs in the United States. Many workers took these concessions as proof that the union was siding with the company. With today's global market in steel, and global ownership of steel mills, the USW waffles between fighting for its workers and keeping their jobs.

Athena, an older worker who has developed strong ties to the union over the years and has served in several elected union offices, observes that union support of gay people and gay visibility are interconnected. *"The union has a civil rights committee. We try to intercede a little bit. But again the union's a good ol' boys' club. It's changing, but it's still a good ol' boys' club. For example, I brought up—they asked what you wanted for contracts, this was the '08 contract. I said I wanted domestic partnership benefits. Their reaction was: you want what? I took it to the USW gentleman who was negotiating our contract, who saw no point in it whatsoever. 'I don't get enough requests for that—there's no point in fighting for it in the contract.' Maybe if you had it, more people would feel comfortable requesting it,"* Athena responded. But there have to be enough visible, vocal people behind a requested change for the union to back it up. Or, there has to be compelling social and political momentum, accompanied by pressure from within.

For example, during the late 1970s, when women occupied the highest number of mill jobs ever, the USW's District 31 ran an influential Women's Caucus. Publishing a regular newsletter from 1977 into the mid-1980s, this caucus mobilized the unions, the courts, and public opinion to argue for female workers' rights, mostly centering around hiring, firing, and pregnancy. They successfully framed sexual harassment as a means to cause division between workers, noting that everyone has the right to make a living safely, and that "a climate of sexual harassment, without recourse, creates conflict within the workforce, diminishing the union's strength" (Fonow 128). A success such as this shows how increasing diversity in a workforce can influence the union to change, but such shifts were curtailed by the shrinking of the steel market, which coincided with the influx of women into the mills and the increased visibility of queers following the Stonewall rebellion (1969). As Ruth Needleman reports, during and after the late 1970s, the big integrated mills lost out to mini-mills, which employ fewer than 200 nonunion workers, and to foreign competition (209). Reflecting on the history of unions in the United States, Needleman observes that early unions relied on exclusion to control wages. Though this shifted to an inclusive model in order to gain members as skilled blue-collar jobs disappeared, it persists in the "tendency to regard white, male experience as universal" (235). Under these circumstances, "unions allowed second-class citizenship status to continue for minority members. The devastating wave of corporate restructuring, downsizing, and capital mobility in the 1980s eliminated tens of thousands of industrial jobs and pulled the rug out from under union based manufacturing" (236).

Though one might imagine that unions would make common cause with queer people and other oppressed groups, since they share a focus on protecting people's rights, this doesn't always happen. Steel unions, specifically, faced devastating challenges at the same moment that queer populations emerged as a vocal political force. And because queers can remain invisible, unlike other minority groups, who are visible to themselves and to outsiders, finding (let alone fighting for) common cause is difficult. Xena reflects: *"I belong to the local union out there, and I've been to a few union meetings. In May of 2010, when I was with my partner of a long time that I married, I wanted to be able to see if I could get her insured. Well I called the union hall and I talked to the woman and she said well you know you'll have to give the company your name, blah, blah, blah, and then it's going to out you and you know, repercussions."* Xena immediately hung up, more a victim of threatened bullying than of actual harassment.

One of the Canadian steelworkers I interviewed makes the point that gay people can't necessarily count on the union in a bittersweet manner. He begins by observing that the union movement *"protects workers, and just being more of a socialist point of view, would eventually lend itself to being supportive of LGBTQ people, and you hear this today. I was just at a Pride ceremony here a few weeks ago, and I spoke on the behalf of this AIDS network I'm on the board of directors of. And the head of the steelworkers union spoke, and he spoke about rights, all human rights. And when human rights are affected in any group, then as an organization that works on people's rights, they're also affected. So they're seeing the links between human rights, and worker's rights, and LGBTQ rights, . . . Now I know people who are in the unions who certainly are openly gay. One other person who spoke at this Pride rally. So you definitely see that more and more."* I asked whether the person who spoke at the Pride rally was a steelworker, since many members of USW and United Steelworkers of Canada locals are in other, unrelated occupations, and learned, *"No he was not, he was a public sector employee. I think the steelworkers are pretty closeted."* Thus, even in Canada, even now, people working in basic steel mills don't find, or seek, union protection from homophobia.

Bernard has been harassed by workers, managers, and everyone in between since he was hired in 1979. He has turned repeatedly to the union and never gotten any satisfaction. He has filed complaints with the EEOC and the ACLU, also without result. He concludes our interview on this poignant note: *"I don't know what to do, but as far as the steel mill goes, when there's a complaint against another worker, you're not supposed to testify against them, you're just supposed to suck it up and let it go. The company and the union are in confidence together. I don't know what else to say."*

In twenty-first-century America, a middle-class, urban, gay, educated audience finds the degree of hostility queer steelworkers display toward their own unions odd, and even paranoid. But anyone who has worked as, or exchanged detailed stories with, a steelworker knows that it is all too real. Allan Bérubé confirmed this situation by acknowledging that even though he had been an out gay activist for decades, "I'm particularly afraid that if older straight union men find out I'm gay, they'll refuse to talk to me and I'll have to go away without hearing their stories" (278). Without question, it's easier to be gay now than it used to be, overall. But for steelworkers, there has been little improvement, and even their unions are a party to the harassment and silencing, rather than a force working against them.

I have often referred to the stereotype that queer people these days are urban, middle-class, and white. As anthropologist Esther Newton puts it, "Homosexual communities are entirely urban and suburban phenomena. They depend on the anonymity and segmentation of metropolitan life" (*Mother Camp* 21). For steelworkers, one component of community is their union. In theory, the union should provide protection, support, and fellowship for all members. Yet, as Newton hints, queer communities work only because they're isolated from work and family, allowing members to remain invisible except to each other. GLBT Steelworkers often seek the protection of this invisibility *within* their unions, meaning that they can't seek, or fight for the right to seek, legal protection using the tools provided by these unions. The separation of sexual identity from work life that characterizes queer sociality makes it difficult for unions to identify and protect their GLBT workers, even if they wanted to.

Unions, like other institutions, reflect the predominant views of society, so in part their responsiveness or lack thereof reflects how far society has come in accepting or accommodating differences. Historically, union resistance to unskilled, female, and minority workers declined as the role of those workers in society expanded and they gained legitimacy at work or in the community. A similar path is emerging in support of gay rights, very slowly and with a reluctance that is more exaggerated in the trades and blue-collar jobs than elsewhere. The AFL-CIO, for example, has a national support organization called Pride at Work. They have developed model contract language to protect domestic partnerships, training modules on homophobia, and an informational film available to constituent unions. The question is, how many unions actually take advantage of these resources, promote Pride at Work, or do trainings that cover all forms of GLBT discrimination? And even when the unions do their best, does the work world of actual gay workers improve?

The USW, for example, includes GLBT antidiscrimination materials in its four-year leadership program, often in the first year. At every national conference, convention, or event, the USW reads its harassment policy paper out loud. Individuals who violate that policy are sent home, with a note to their district director. The Canadian Steelworkers union has gone a bit further than their U.S. counterpart, in part because women play a more central role in the leadership. Every local is supposed to have a civil rights and a Women of Steel committee, and each district has a civil rights coordinator. However, these committees have less power than, say, a grievance committee or a bargaining committee, and some locals make little use of them.

Further, the contract under which most basic steelworkers are employed does not include protections based on "sexual orientation" or "gender identity" or any other category under which queers might fall. Protected groups, according to the current contract, which was adopted in 2008, are listed in Article Four, Section A, entitled "Non-discrimination." It reads, in full, "The provisions of this agreement shall be applied to all employees without regard to: (a) race, color, religious creed, national origin, disability, veterans disability or status as a veteran; or (b) sex or age, except where sex or age is a bona fide occupational qualification; or (c) citizenship or immigration status, except as permitted by law" (55). The process of revising this contract was finalized and the contract was reapproved in 2012, but the language about discrimination, and the protected categories remain unchanged.

Certainly, gay people are not uniformly hostile toward steelworkers' unions. Many narrators love their unions and feel welcome there; most understand that the union has been responsible for numerous benefits and for countless improvements in the workplace, including those related to health and safety. While a substantial number may consider the unions pointless, expensive, or impotent, the union's historic role in making steelwork a high-paying and safer job would be hard to ignore. While some queer steelworkers feel more acknowledged on the shop floor than they do at the union hall, others run for, and are elected to, important positions within the union, whose role they staunchly defend.

My narrators reflect a variety of knowledge about, reactions to, and support for the unions. Some have taken labor studies classes, and are proud of the progress that unions have made on behalf of American workers. Many understand the insight that Allan Bérubé identified in the gay members of the Marine Cooks and Stewards Union "that the only real change will come out of a solidarity that can reach across and dismantle the hierarchies of race, class, gender, and sexuality—a solidarity that can engage intellectuals, activists, working people, and artists in its struggle" (259). These people's lives disrupt the myths that gay people are not working-class and that unions are for straight people.

Unions, Power, Progress

Union leaders are elected by the membership. Those with the most votes (and, by implication, the most mainstream views) win. Some minority representation occurs when unions run slates of candidates, which is how the first women and African Americans gained entry to leadership. Throughout the 1960s, African Americans organized within the USW for representation (in the Ad Hoc Committee of Black Steelworkers). By the 1970s, Chicanos and women had begun challenging the old majority. The district in Northwest Indiana (then District 31) had the first women's organization as well as a black caucus. During this period, however, I can find no mention in union literature of the rights of GLBT workers.

Historically, of course, unions protected members of the dominant group (native-born straight white men) and set policies to favor them. Any griever or shop steward who defended an unpopular policy or, worse, an unpopular worker, might not have been reelected. Hierarchical structures and "old boy" networks created almost insurmountable barriers for minorities seeking to gain leadership positions. Add in complicated election procedures and the need to be slated, and it becomes clear why so many unions often do not protect queers.

According to Mary Margaret Fonow's *Union Women*, published in 2003, there's a long-standing tension within the unions between the unique needs of specific groups of workers and the drive for solidarity. Too much branching out into subgroups is perceived as placing the unifying force of the movement in jeopardy (86). When the economy is bad and jobs are scarce, the union wants economic issues to trump all others. This view created sharp divisions in the early 1980s during the restructuring of steel. During this period, women and workers of color found themselves most vulnerable to layoffs for two reasons: for women, they were the last hired; For blacks and other workers of color, they held the worst jobs in steelmaking, which were the ones often eliminated by new technology. The voices of GLBT workers were inaudible, as thousands of workers lost employment, creating a climate in which no one wanted to take risks. As the U.S. steel industry collapsed, the union, to keep any jobs at all, made concessions that workers resented, which further eroded support for unions even from their own rank-and-file members.

Political and social support for unions had already been eroding among Americans when Reagan fired striking air traffic controllers in 1981. Steel unions faced stiff competition from more modern mills in other countries, along with restructuring (wherein technological improvements reduced the number of workers needed in each mill). One strategy unions used to regain popular opinion and unify the ranks was to call for class unity, which to some degree marginalized workers with specific demands. The theory behind unionism is that if everyone agrees to act as one, management can't single out or punish particular people; the greater the unity, the greater the power. Historically, unfortunately, unions also promoted exclusion over inclusion, though the excluded actually made up the majority of workers: immigrants, women, blacks, and unskilled labor.

Within unions, minorities and reformers experience a tension between being dissidents and identifying with the mainstream "straighter path of trying to survive and find work in an increasingly hostile environment" (La-Tour 26). Like their unions, in times of crisis beleaguered minority workers often close ranks behind the union instead of fighting for their own particular issues. Those that resist this impulse get no support from their unions. My interviews repeatedly showed that when queer steelworkers were willing to file complaints (which is unusual), the union often did little or nothing to help them succeed. In the current global context, as Bernard points out, many union stewards and grievers fear rocking the boat, especially when an issue does not affect the majority. They thus join management in looking the other way, believing that this keeps the core group of "mainstream" steelworkers happy. It's no coincidence that LaTour describes the unions as choosing a "straighter path."

Epilogue

My neighborhood in Gary has a regular pot-luck party facetiously called "Homos in the Hood." I was discussing my research there one evening with a gay educator—the sort of middle-class white male who exemplifies queers in America. He was shocked and disbelieving that work at the mills is *still* fraught with harassment, fear, and violence for queer folks. Even when another person joined our conversation, stating that he had worked in the mills for twenty plus years and that my observations were accurate, the educator could not seem to accept them. He asked whether the problem might be with steelworker anxiety—fear of rejection, or insecurity. In his experience, when people have the courage to come out, they improve their quality of life and pave the way for other queers in their vicinity. Though he did ultimately accept, based on first-person testimony, that this strategy might not be effective in the mills, he was clearly still struggling, unable to fit his experience of being gay in an alienating but ultimately accepting time and place with what he was learning about the mills.

When one perspective within a culture comes to define the culture, other perspectives are invisible. Queers have fought hard and long for the progress we have experienced, and our dominant narrative of gradual progress toward freedom makes it hard to notice pockets of stasis, or even regression. Bernard uses humor and understatement to undermine the dominant narrative of queer progress: *"I went to the labor pool. And I have had no problem there. That's the first place I have had no problem with the other workers. Including the lady that called me an abomination, but she liked me because I can be mouthy when it's necessary to be mouthy."* Being called an abomination doesn't fit my description of a problem-free workplace, though being "mouthy" certainly fits the queer stereotype. Our search for pride and progress can't blind us to the complicated, messy, bitingly funny experiences of mill workers and other working-class queers, which complicate our understanding of what it means to be queer. Further, the kind of sex and pleasure people have within the space of the mill challenges what it means to be queer everywhere. Finally, the consistent violence and danger

USX as seen from Miller Beach, 2012. Photograph by Patrick Bytnar.

of gay working-class life in (and out of) the mill needs to be a part of how we understand queer identity and sexuality.

After hearing stories from mill workers in and around Gary about how being gay makes mill work that much harder, I began to wonder whether the situation is better in Canada. Several basic steel mills still function in Canada, though, as in the United States, the steel industry there is only a fraction of its former self. Yet Canada has a vastly more tolerant social and political climate. Gay marriage passed there nationally with minimal opposition, same-sex spousal benefits are guaranteed, and workplace non-discrimination legislation includes sexual orientation. This acceptance is reflected in the Steelworkers Union. The USW's web page for Canada includes a link to "Steel Pride," which states: "Steelworkers are helping to raise understanding and respect for the diversity and differences that make us strong, proud and, indeed, Everybody's Union" (http://www.USW.ca/union/pride?id=0003). The Toronto Pride parade has a large United Steelworkers of Canada (USWC) contingent each year. How does this federal and union policy trickle down into the rank and file of Canadian steelworkers? In some ways, Canada is a different world, but in most ways, basic steel working conditions mirrored those that steelworkers experience in Gary.

Carolyn Egan, a USWC organizer working in Toronto, told me several stories that reflected a growing acceptance for LGBT working people in the culture as a whole. For example, she described one very traditional, old school official in the USWC who had struggled when his son came out. Yet his relationship with his son outweighed his bigotry, and he wound up giving a speech at a union event about accepting gay laborers and working-class people. This speech then became a very popular replay on YouTube. In another instance, the USWC had organized workers at a light manufacturing plant in Toronto, where a woman was receiving constant harassment for perceived lesbianism. Union interventions were ineffective at stopping this behavior, and the employee eventually killed herself. At her funeral, attended by large numbers of her co-workers, there was a general sense that she had been gay-bashed to death, and outcry from the rank and file led to her supervisor's dismissal.

Though these stories illustrate a general cultural acceptance of queer working people, they don't contain any actual out and proud workers, let alone steelworkers. The Steel Pride group advertised on the web has no members, nor does it have anyone working for it, and the contingent at the Toronto Pride parade consists largely of supportive straight people, few if any of whom are blue-collar workers. Carolyn did remember a steelworker from Hamilton who regularly came up to march with them, but he never revealed his name. And no one in the union hall remembered instances when GLBT steelworkers filed grievances about workplace discrimination or harassment because of sexual orientation—the same response I got in the United States.

Therefore, in Canada I met steelworkers through the same methods I had established at home—I told everyone what I was doing, and tried everything they suggested. For example, when I called to reserve a B and B for my visit, the motherly proprietor asked what brought me to Hamilton, and I told her. And that's where the cultural acceptance was first noticeable. Instead of getting quiet or hostile, she gave me the name and email address of a columnist who often wrote about gay issues for the local paper. When I contacted the columnist, she wrote a short blurb preceding my visit. In Hamilton, I went to bookstores, and asked at the labor museum. Though everyone was friendly, and there was less incredulity than I get when I discuss my work in the United States, the steelworkers themselves were still hidden. Those that contacted me carried the burden of secrecy and fear I recognized from my American narrators, and their workplace experiences were no different.

Contrast within Canada is dramatic. In Toronto, I wandered through the gay village, which had bars, pride flags, sex toy shops—all the usual accoutrements of the urban gay lifestyle. Yet Hamilton, the working-class "steel town," has only one gay bar. Because I take my research so seriously, I decided to stop by when one of my narrators invited me. I wrote down the bar's name, glanced at a map, and drove down there, but then couldn't locate it. I wound up coming back to the B and B and getting the address and specific instructions off the internet. I returned and scoured the proper street, finally finding a storefront with no name, address, lights, or entrance. A small handwritten sign said "Enter through the back." As I wandered down unfamiliar alleys at night, all I could think was, "My mother would not approve of this . . ." The back was lit, had signage, and by the end of the evening was quite crowded—the bar itself was huge. I asked why it was so concealed, and people said that patrons don't want to be seen entering, and that most gay clubs that have opened in Hamilton eventually close because the rents skyrocket when the nature of the business becomes obvious. Though Hamilton is a growing city, whose working-class industrial base is being replaced by companies that focus on health care and education, it still provides limited tolerance for gay people. And this in Canada, which I thought would be so different.

Three steelworkers agreed to be interviewed in Hamilton, all white men, though one is a "dresser" who usually presents as a woman. Two remained carefully closeted during their time at the mill, while Larry/Lisa would have preferred closeting to the harassment and violence that became a constant part of her work and social life. Since Larry was laid off a few years ago, being gay and "a dresser" has gotten easier—she notes that the people working at the café where we talked see her in both genders, and are welcoming and relaxed about it. But *at work I got ridiculed. About wearing bras, and panties, and dressing up. It went on for, I'm not kidding, twenty-five years. I mean really bad stuff. . . . Had my locker broken into, my tools ripped off, little notes stuffed into my locker, and everything else. I lived with it.*" By email, following our talk, Lisa added, *"I was mugged and beaten up three times. . . . And yet I would always keep my head up and try and carry on my life the way I wanted to."*

Lisa emphasizes this last statement throughout her story. Verbal and physical abuse were constant, her first love died of AIDS and her second of diabetes complications, and many transgender people she met committed suicide. Ultimately, she decided not to go through with gender reassignment surgery, fearing rejection and depression. Yet she is always smiling, proud, and positive about her past and future. A turning point came when she told her son about her "dressing," and he responded with acceptance and love. The son wrote a poem that he delivered at an open-mic event as a surprise for Lisa, who says she cried shamelessly when she heard it. The poem, called "Breaking the Silence," tells the story of Lisa's life, including a section on the mills:

> The hatred grew outside his home
> Bathrooms at work
> Littered with poems
> They called him a fag
> And attacked his own
> And with cracks of bones
> Tongue-lashed over the phone
> Blasts thrash like pelting stones
> Into the trash he was mentally thrown
> But for 33 years
> Day after day after day . . .
> he had shown
> with his head held high
> and his wounds neatly sewn
> denying with silence
> his cover not blown
> within himself
> but low
> low
> and alone.

Lisa's story, with a full-page photo, appeared in the *Hamilton Spectator* on May 23, 2007, and she has appeared on a local TV news magazine, and in the *United Church Observer* (November 2007). All this openness, including permission for me to use her real name, print photos, and quote from her son's poem, is unusual for a gay steelworker.

Yet Lisa's story is a fitting place to conclude because she raises issues of identity, narrative, and progress. To an extent, all people are constituted by the series of stories we tell about ourselves. That's how memory, identity, and context are structured. This is even more true for queer people, since we mostly don't grow up in families that teach us what we are and how that works—instead, that's something we create through a series of heard and told stories. For example, coming out is a well-known theme in the narrative that structures gay life. Therefore when someone like Lisa tells

Lisa in the woods, passing time with nature, ca. 2010. Courtesy of Larry/Lisa Stroud.

me her story, it's an act of trust, generosity, and intimacy. Lisa shares her story as widely as possible, not only because she is justly proud of what she has accomplished, but also because she wants to help the many people who remain silent and scared. In contrast, many narrators told me things they had never revealed before. To anyone.

While it is true that one could construe individual testimonies/oral histories as being in cahoots with neoliberal discourses of individualism and that narrators' words do not exist outside of discourse in general or outside of structures of power, it is also true that individuals *do* have agency in their own lives and telling one's story can lead to a *collective* movement. People in general, and my narrators specifically, tell stories to pull themselves together—to make sense of their identity—and to form community. Each queer steelworker, as I told them there were others and that specific details of their experience were shared by a larger community, felt less alone. Though they have not met one another, just knowing that each was not an isolated individual but rather part of a collective, however invisible, raised a weight off their shoulders.

The invisibility of queer people, or at least its potential, makes community harder. When African Americans and then women were hired in at the mills in the 1960s and 1970s, they faced opposition and violence. In each case, collective action was difficult, but allies could readily be visually identified, and fair treatment could be fought for, if not necessarily won. Gay people don't have that automatic community.

Further, as earlier chapters demonstrate, the danger and isolation of mill work bind the workers together into a community that feels rewarding—almost like a family. And queer steelworkers (provided they remain invisible and unpoliticized) can partake of that community. Why would they trade that bond for an imaginary identification with fellow queers who they can't necessarily relate to and might not even like? The middle-class idea of coming out as a brave step designed to create community and reach out to others just does not apply to these queer steelworkers, whose closeting is what enables their important, empowering work family. Athena explains: *"The mills are a world of its own. You <she said to me> worked on cars. You were a car mechanic. You could hold your tools in your hands, am I right? Many of our tools you can't hold in your hands. They're huge. You need a crane to move things around. Mills historically are dangerous. . . . It's dirty, it's hot, it's cold. You're working at heights—you're working with everything large in the mill. Nothing is on a small scale. And everything is pretty much dangerous. . . . The mills are hard on your body. Physically. You ever seen any of the videos or anything? On steelmaking? It is hard on your body. Guys are crawling in and out of little holes—cubby holes, and in and out of stuff. Into tanks. Climbing up high. Do steel mills have fatalities? Yes. Do we have a lot of routine injuries? Yes. Lots of slips, trips, and falls. Winter kills us, with the snow and the ice. And again, we sit on the lake, so you've got wind. You could put all the salt out you want, and that floor could still be slick. We have a lot of foreign bodies to the eyes, even though the guys all have safety glasses, and they wear them. You still get some of that. You still get pinch points—machine guarding. Now remember, the mill is old. The equipment is old. I think our newest production line is in the 60s. But if a guy says he wants a respirator to do a certain job, he gets it. [But they don't.] It's the old culture of things. They are tough, and they don't need it.*

"The region is not [gay friendly]. No, the region is not. And that's probably why a lot of people don't want to [come out]. You have to rely on your co-workers in the steel mill. You not only have to rely on you—you have to rely on them. And in the back of your mind, are you thinking, if something happens, are they gonna turn their back. 'Cause they kinda wish you were dead anyway? It's a regional thing. It's a cultural thing. It's . . .

"So that's part of the problem. I've had people ask me: Have you ever been to the parade? Is it a party? Is it everything we see on TV? Yeah, it is, it's a big

party, and it's a lot of fun—you want to come? Ah, no. But yeah you have to rely on your co-workers out there, that you are like them, or they like you. I think some people are leery, and their own spouses don't know, let alone their co-workers. There are some married gay people." Linking scale, danger, masculine posing, and secrecy about nonnormative sexuality, this story demonstrates how storytelling makes an imaginary queer community possible, since identity and community arise from a sense of shared experience, especially shared oppression.

That sense of community deriving, at least in part, from shared oppression is one reason why queer steelworkers don't leave their jobs, in spite of the danger they face there, and the silencing and harassment they experience. After reading their stories, one may well wonder why the steelworkers don't seek out a more welcoming work situation. One answer is that, since mills recruit new workers through referrals from current workers, the jobs tend to cross generational lines within families. Wanda is one of many narrators who fit this pattern—she is a third generation USX employee. As in military families, the danger and stress of the work becomes a source of pride—there's almost a cult of masculine sacrifice. Lesbians gain status by participating in this tradition, and gay men, otherwise concerned with disappointing their families by failing to fill traditional masculine roles, may cling to mill jobs for approval. Though queer folks are marginalized—and often invisible—within this culture, it still can provide them access to a meaningful sense of identity, belonging, and purpose. In addition, it can't be forgotten that areas such as Northwest Indiana offer workers without higher education very few forms of employment with salary levels and benefits comparable to those in the steel industry. There is no comparison to steelworker pay in retail, the service industry, or even the ubiquitous casinos.

All of the people I interviewed had arrived at a place in their life where they could tell me their story of being a gay steelworker. Identifying themselves this way enabled them to make sense of their experiences, feelings, and pleasures. The label placed them within a community, a context, which made them intelligible to themselves. Though almost always silent at work about this identification, and often silent about it in every other setting, naming themselves and telling their stories was a powerful and empowering step.

Scholars or students of queer history and identity in the United States need to hear and honor these stories. As Eve Sedgwick points out, whom we have or want to have sex with does not affect much of our daily life or our work. Yet sexual orientation, as a means of defining who we are, affects everything. Lisa is a gay man looking for a long-term, loving partner. Until a few years ago, she was also a steelworker. She, and the thirty-nine other people I interviewed, demonstrate how intertwined sexual orientation, work, and gender expression are. Stories like these, about people in all regions of the country, in all types of jobs, are crucial to understanding what it means to be queer.

APPENDIX

The Narrators

Though I met and spoke to many gay, lesbian, and transgender steelworkers, and countless other steelworkers who would not have identified themselves as queer, only the forty narrators who signed consent forms are listed here. Each is identified by an alias, and I provide as much information as I can without compromising the narrator's confidentiality. I also give the date of our interview, which occurred in my office unless otherwise specified. Transcriptions of all the interviews are stored in the Human Sexuality Collection/Archive at Cornell University.

1. Andy, interviewed on November 15, 2009, at a bar. A young (thirties?) man with a military buzz cut, casually dressed, and friendly with the bar regulars. He told his stories with panache and pride.

2. Ben, interviewed on November 23, 2009. He was a big guy in his thirties, with a jocular, confiding manner. Though he appeared relaxed, he also kept a careful distance. He wore jeans and a T-shirt and had a prominent gut, which he occasionally adjusted for comfort.

3. Chris, interviewed at his house on January 15, 2010. He was very sick, and using a walker. Though wearing a T-shirt, pajama pants, and a bathrobe, he still looked dignified and proper. He had a very neat, tasteful home, and seemed to find attention disconcerting. He smiled sweetly, disarming in one so ill, when I asked about his partner.

4. Dave, interviewed on January 16, 2010, at his home. He was thin and neat, with a scrupulously kept, densely decorated house. In his forties or fifties.

5. Erin, interviewed in January 2010. A bit sloping in the shoulders and tentative in her demeanor. She wore an embroidered V-neck sweater. Probably in her early fifties.

6. Fern, interviewed on January 29, 2010. She was a slim Asian woman with short, spiked hair and a ready, flirtatious smile. Though tiny, she had a butch swagger to her walk and told stories revealing an intense pride in her work. I would guess she was in her mid-thirties.

7. Gail, interviewed on January 25, 2010. She is a short, stocky woman with neat gray hair. She wore blue jeans and a denim shirt advertising ISG (International Steel Group, the former owner of her mill). She had a warm smile and laughing eyes, and loved to tell stories. She was about sixty.

8. Harriet, interviewed on April 10, 2010. She is mixed Indian and Mexican, and very butch. She had black, feathered hair, and seemed to be in her late forties. Her boots and leather jacket had many zippers.

9. Isabel, interviewed in June 2010. Younger (mid-twenties) than most of the narrators, with a presentation somewhere between hipster and goth. She was skinny, with hair partly black and partly hot pink. Clearly not comfortable in Northwest Indiana, she fantasized about moving elsewhere.

10. Jay, interviewed on July 11, 2010, in his home. Though incredibly small, his apartment was nicely decorated and included an electronic dog, of which he was quite proud. He had curly, close-cropped hair, and looked to be just under fifty, with a wide torso and neck. He had a warm, genuine smile, complete with dimples. Earrings and a carefully ironed shirt were the only hints of gayness.

11. Keith, interviewed in July 2010, was young (under twenty). He had short dark hair and a stocky build. In a T-shirt and jeans, he seemed unremarkable and matter-of-fact.

12. Lakisha, interviewed in August 2010 at a bar in Chicago. She was slight, with clipped sentences and diction, though she relaxed as we continued to talk. Maybe in her mid-forties, she is blonde and delicate-featured.

13. Miles, interviewed on August 19, 2010, at the Cornwall Iron Furnace, a museum slightly west of Philadelphia. He is a stocky, bearded man who brought to the interview a picnic that he insisted on sharing with me. He wore cargo shorts and a Steelers T-shirt. He had begun attending college and was eager to discuss that, as well as his experiences in steel.

14. Nate, interviewed on August 28, 2010, at his home. He is an older, dignified but incredibly friendly man. He was thrilled to have a chance to share his stories, including a very detailed account of the commitment ceremony he planned with his late partner. He had a neatly trimmed goatee and wore Pride jewelry. His current partner had cooked a very elegant lunch and "plated" it before leaving us alone. During the (long!) interview, the partner washed my car. I've never felt so welcome in such a short time.

15. Olshana, interviewed on August 29, 2010, at a coffee shop. Probably in her mid-fifties, she looked and talked like a hippie radical leftist.

16. Phil, interviewed in December 2010. I Facebook stalked him, guessing he was gay and worked at a mill based on comments he wrote on the walls of friends of mine who were steelworkers. He wore a baseball hat, hoodie, jeans, and work boots. With his beard and wild hair, he seemed out of place anywhere indoors, yet he had a disarmingly soft voice, and generous stories.

17. Quentin, interviewed on February 12, 2011, in a restaurant. Though the place was loud, he usually spoke to me with his hand over his mouth, as though he couldn't bear to be heard. He smoked constantly, looked run-down and scruffy, and was probably in his early fifties.

18. Renee, interviewed January 29, 2011. She wore an Indiana University sweatshirt and jeans. Though butch, she was not aggressively so.

19. Scott, interviewed on 26 January 2011. He was tall and substantially built, but fit. He had a white, neatly trimmed beard and wore a hunting shirt. He was well into his sixties.

20. Tommy, interviewed on January 26, 2011, at his home in a trailer park. He had a long mustache, and wore a sweatshirt and camouflage baseball hat. He was visibly nervous and held a small black dog with white paws and a pink rhinestone collar, which he petted constantly. He was probably in his forties, and was thin and wiry.

21. Undine, interviewed on February 12, 2011. She was nervous, and didn't want to be recorded. Though at first subdued and hesitant, she later relaxed, displaying one dimple and warm eyes. She was a tall, dishwater blonde woman with wiry, cowboy legs.

22. Victor, interviewed on January 28, 2011, in a bar. He was a very heavy man with several missing teeth, yet he still managed to have a sweet, completely distracting smile. He wore a military hat representing his rank, and a back support (lifting) belt.

23. Wanda, interviewed on January 26, 2011. She wore a scrupulously butch tie, sweater, and hat, along with a Bluetooth. She was a dark-complected black woman with no visible hair. Her handshake and manner of sitting established butch dominance immediately, as did her sideways, knowing smile. I would guess she was in her mid to late thirties.

24. Xena, interviewed January 31, 2011, at her home. She wore a Steelers jersey over a thermal shirt and smoked constantly. She had a dry sense of humor and a butch presentation. She had iron gray hair. Probably in her mid-forties.

25. Yesenia, interviewed on February 11, 2011. A Latina wearing a Notre Dame fleece and black eyeliner, she had a cute smile and told a great story.

26. Zach, interviewed on February 9, 2011. He was a quiet, unobtrusive man in a black T-shirt and a mill uniform jacket. Big, but gentle and thoughtful in tone.

27. Athena, interviewed February 16, 2011. She often paused and looked appraisingly at the recorder. Sometimes, she asked me to turn it off. She wore glasses and had a middle-aged body, thick, especially in the middle. Probably somewhere in her forties or fifties.

28. Bernard, interviewed March 23, 2011. He was a medium-complected black man, with neat hair but messy clothes. His voice sometimes got very loud, as if his own stories angered him. When his mannerisms approached queenliness, he would make eye contact and smile. In his early sixties.

29. Carmen, interviewed in March 2011. In her fifties, she is a black woman with dreadlocks, who has some scarring from a burn accident at the mill. She was very reserved and held her lower jaw tensely.

30. Danielle, interviewed on April 25, 2011. She is a big woman, with long, straight, almost stringy hair. She wore glasses and dressed casually but with lots of makeup.

31. Elise, interviewed July 18, 2011, in her home. She is a small woman, with vast sums of nervous energy. She smoked without stopping, and talked quickly, with

many unexpected topic changes. She seemed strung out and paranoid. She had many missing teeth, and other health problems, including very bad eyesight, which made signing the consent form difficult.

32. Fred chose this alias when I interviewed him on 4 February 2011, at a restaurant. He had red, glittery nails, three rings per finger, large teased hair, long feather earrings, and a mustache and goatee. He was painfully thin and wore all black. He loved to talk and held my attention for hours. He was clearly a regular at the restaurant, and the servers knew and liked him.

33. Larry/Lisa, interviewed July 9, 2011, at a restaurant in Canada. I have kept her original name, with her permission, which explains why she doesn't follow my alphabetical naming pattern. She was "dressed" when we met, at a public place near her home. She wore jeans decorated with rhinestone flowers, and a blouse. Her hair and makeup were impeccable. Even when she described abuse and tragedy, such as the long strike currently on at one of the steel mills in Hamilton, she emphasized support and possibility.

34. Hugo, interviewed July 10, 2011, at the gallery he owns in Canada. He is identifiable but not obvious as a gay man. His hair is short and neat, his body is substantial, and his bearing and voice are interested and engaged. I liked him immediately, and he enjoyed telling stories of the mill and the town around it.

35. Ian, interviewed July 10, 2011, at a restaurant in Canada. A fun-loving, easy-to-talk-to, working-class guy. He had receding gray hair and an easy acceptance of other people and circumstances. Probably in his fifties, he clearly had learned not to take anything too seriously.

36. Janis, interviewed July 20, 2011, at a restaurant. She wore the jacket of union electrical workers and identified as a strong union supporter. Blonde and fit, in her fifties, she had a lively demeanor, but she refused to be recorded.

37. Kate, interviewed in August 2011, at a bar. Relaxed and funny, she loved to talk and was full of stories about the area, the mill, family, and life. She carried herself with confidence and had a physical presence. She had medium-length gray-blonde hair.

38. Lupe, interviewed September 18, 2011, at a bar. She was fairly boxy in build, with short black hair and butch mannerisms. Though she was in her mid-forties, there was something very boyish and innocent about her.

39. Marie, interviewed October 19, 2011, at a coffee shop in Pittsburgh. She was an older woman, many years beyond the steel mill, which showed in her body and demeanor. She had medium length hair, wore jewelry and a blazer, and was probably in her sixties. When she discussed her life as a steelworker, memories began to flood back, and a butch attitude accompanied them.

40. Norman, interviewed December 9, 2011, at a coffee shop. He is an older man (sixties?) with flamboyant mannerisms and the presentation of a gentleman.

Works Cited

Allison, Dorothy. *Skin: Talking About Sex, Class and Literature*. Ithaca: Firebrand Books, 1994.

Appleby, George Alan. "Ethnographic Study of Gay and Bisexual Working-Class Men in the United States." *Journal of Gay and Lesbian Social Services* 12.3/4 (2001): 51–62.

Badgett, M. V. Lee. *Money, Myths, and Change: The Economic Lives of Lesbians and Gay Men*. Chicago: University of Chicago Press, 2001.

Badgett, M. V. Lee, and Mary C. King. "Lesbian and Gay Occupational Strategies." In *Homo Economics: Capitalism, Community, and Lesbian and Gay Life*, edited by Amy Gluckman and Betsy Reed, 73–86. New York: Routledge, 1997.

Bérubé, Allan. *My Desire for History: Essays in Gay, Community, and Labor History*. Edited with an introduction by John D'Emilio and Estelle B. Freedman. Chapel Hill: University of North Carolina Press, 2011.

Boyd, Nan Alamilla. "Who Is the Subject?: Queer Theory Meets Oral History." *Journal of the History of Sexuality* 17.2 (May 2008): 177–89.

Carter, Julie Hope. "Who Cares if Barbie Loves Midge, As Long As They Get the Dreamhouse?: Poor and Working Class Lesbians of the New Millennium." *Educational Studies* 29.4 (1998): 410–33.

Catano, James V. *Ragged Dicks: Masculinity, Steel, and the Rhetoric of the Self-Made Man*. Carbondale: Southern Illinois University Press, 2001.

Chauncey, George. *Gay New York: Gender, Urban Culture, and the Making of the Gay Male World, 1890–1940*. New York: Basic Books, 1994.

Clarkson, Jay. "'Everyday Joe' versus 'Prissy, Bitchy, Queens': Gay Masculinity on StraightActing.com." *Journal of Men's Studies* 14.2 (Spring 2006): 191–207.

Clemens, Paul. *Punching Out: One Year in a Closing Auto Plant*. New York: Anchor, 2011.

Connell, R. W. *The Men and the Boys*. St. Leonards, Australia: Allen & Unwin, 2000.

Davich, Jerry. "Wanted: Gay, lesbian, bisexual steelworkers." *Northwest Indiana Post-Tribune*, January 24, 2011, 5.

Deaux, Kay, and Joseph C. Ullman. *Women of Steel: Female Blue-Collar Workers in the Basic Steel Industry*. New York: Praeger, 1983.

D'Emilio, John. *Sexual Politics, Sexual Communities: The Making of a Homosexual Minority in the United States, 1940–1970*. 2nd edition. Chicago: University of Chicago Press, 1998.

———. *The World Turned: Essays on Gay History, Politics, and Culture*. Durham: Duke University Press, 2002.

Dorson, Richard M. *Land of the Millrats*. Cambridge: Harvard University Press, 1981.

Embrick, David G., Carol S. Walther, and Corrine M. Wickens. "Working Class Masculinity: Keeping Gay Men and Lesbians Out of the Workplace." *Sex Roles* 56 (2007): 757–66.

Faue, Elizabeth. "Gender, Class, and History." In *New Working Class Studies*, edited by John Russo and Sherry Lee Linkon, 19–31. Ithaca: ILR Press, 2005.

Flanders, Laura. "Queer Issues Are Class Issues: Where Next for the LGBTQ Movement?" http://www.thenation.com/blog/168586/queer-issues-are-class-issues-where-next-lgbtq-movement.

Fonow, Mary Margaret. *Union Women: Forging Feminism in the United Steelworkers of America*. Minneapolis: University of Minnesota Press, 2003.

Friskopp, Annette, and Sharon Silverstein. *Straight Jobs, Gay Lives: Gay and Lesbian Professionals, the Harvard Business School, and the American Work Place*. New York: Scribner, 1995.

Grele, Ronald J., with Studs Terkel et al. *Envelopes of Sound: The Art of Oral History*. 2nd edition, revised and expanded. New York: Praeger, 1991.

Halberstam, Judith. *Female Masculinity*. Durham: Duke University Press, 1998.

———. *In a Queer Time and Place: Transgender Bodies, Subcultural Lives*. New York: New York University Press, 2005.

Hall, Christopher. *Steel Phoenix: The Rise and Fall of the U.S. Steel Industry*. New York: Palgrave Macmillan, 1997.

The Heat: Steelworker Lives and Legends. Mena, Ark.: Cedar Hill Publications, 2001.

Herring, Scott. *Another Country: Queer Anti-Urbanism*. New York: New York University Press, 2010.

Hollibaugh, Amber L. *My Dangerous Desires: A Queer Girl Dreaming Her Way Home*. Durham: Duke University Press, 2000.

Howard, John. *Men Like That: A Southern Queer History*. Chicago: University of Chicago Press, 1999.

Hunt, Gerald, and Monica Bielski Boris. "The Lesbian, Gay, Bisexual, and Transgender Challenge to American Labor." In *The Sex of Class: Women Transforming American Labor*, edited by Dorothy Sue Cobble, 81–98. Ithaca: Cornell University Press, 2007.

Johnson, E. Patrick. *Sweet Tea: Black Gay Men of the South*. Chapel Hill: University of North Carolina Press, 2008.

Kennedy, Elizabeth Lapovsky. "Telling Tales: Oral History and the Construction of Pre-Stonewall Lesbian Identity." In *The Oral History Reader*, edited by Robert Perks and Alistair Thomson, 344–55. London: Routledge, 1998.

Kennedy, Elizabeth Lapovsky, and Madeline E. Davis. *Boots of Leather, Slippers of Gold: The History of a Lesbian Community*. New York: Penguin, 1993.

Kinsey, Alfred C., Wardell B. Pomeroy, and Clyde E. Martin. *Sexual Behavior in the Human Male*. Philadelphia: Saunders, 1948.

Krupat, Kitty. *Out At Work: Building a Gay-Labor Alliance*. Minneapolis: University of Minnesota Press, 2001.

Lane, James B. "Gary's First Hundred Years: A Centennial History of Gary, Indiana 1906–2006." *Steel Shavings* 37 (2006).

————, ed. "Calumet Regional Steelworkers' Tales." *Steel Shavings* 19 (1990).

LaTour, Jane. *Sisters in the Brotherhoods: Working Women Organizing for Equality in New York*. New York: Palgrave Macmillan, 2008.

Lipsky, Laura van Dernoot, with Connie Burk. *Trauma Stewardship: An Everyday Guide to Caring for Self While Caring for Others*. Seattle: Las Olas Press, 2007.

Luxton, Meg, and June Corman. *Getting by in Hard Times: Gendered Labor at Home and on the Job*. Toronto, University of Toronto Press, 2001.

Martin, Molly, ed. *Hard-Hatted Women: Stories of Struggle and Success in the Trades*. Seattle: Seal Press, 1988.

Matthews, Robert Guy. "The Lonely Life of a Steelworker." *Wall Street Journal Online*, 30 June, 2003.

McShane, Steven G., and Gary S. Wilk. *Steel Giants: Historic Images from the Calumet Regional Archives*. Bloomington: Indiana University Press, 2009.

Moss, William W. "Oral History: What Is It and Where Did It Come From?" In *The Past Meets the Present: Essays on Oral History*, edited by David Stricklin and Rebecca Sharpless, 5–14. Lanham, Md.: University Press of America, 1988.

National LGBT Cancer Network. "Barriers to Health Care." http://www.cancer-network.org/cancer_information/cancer_and_the_lgbt_community/barriers_to_lgbt_healthcare.php. August 22, 2013.

Needleman, Ruth. *Black Freedom Fighters in Steel: The Struggle for Democratic Unionism*. Ithaca: Cornell University Press, 2003.

Newton, Esther. *Cherry Grove, Fire Island: Sixty Years in America's First Gay and Lesbian Town*. Boston: Beacon Press, 1993.

————. *Margaret Mead Made Me Gay: Personal Essays, Public Ideas*. Durham: Duke University Press, 2000.

————. *Mother Camp: Female Impersonators in America*. 1972. Reprint. Chicago: University of Chicago Press, 1979.

Olson, Carol. *Wives of Steel: Voices of Women from the Sparrows Point Steelmaking Communities*. University Park: Pennsylvania State University Press, 2005.

Rapoport, Rhona, et al. *Beyond Work-Family Balance: Advancing Gender Equity and Workplace Performance*. San Francisco: Jossey-Bass, 2002.

Rubin, Lillian Breslow. *Worlds of Pain: Life in the Working-Class Family*. New York: Basic Books, 1976.

Rudacille, Deborah. *Roots of Steel: Boom and Bust in an American Mill Town*. New York: Pantheon, 2010.

Sedgwick, Eve Kosofsky. *Epistemology of the Closet*. Updated edition. Berkeley: University of California Press, 2008.

Serrin, William. *Homestead: The Glory and Tragedy of an American Steel Town*. New York: Vintage, 1992.

Terkel, Studs. *Working: People Talk About What They Do All Day and How They Feel About What They Do*. 1974. Reprint. New York: MJF Books, 2004.

Thompson, Paul. *The Voice of the Past: Oral History*. 3rd edition. Oxford: Oxford University Press, 2000.

Vukmir, Rade B. *The Mill*. Urbana: University of Illinois Press, 1999.

Walshok, Mary Lindenstein. *Blue-Collar Women: Pioneers on the Male Frontier*. Garden City, N.Y.: Anchor Books, 1981.

Warner, Michael. *The Trouble with Normal: Sex, Politics, and the Ethics of Queer Life*. Cambridge: Harvard University Press, 1999.

Warren, James. "Alice Puerala, 58, Steel Union Leader." *Chicago Tribune*, online edition, June 21, 1986.

———. "Alice Puerala Regains Reins of Steel Union Local." *Chicago Tribune*, online edition, May 1, 1985.

Wymard, Ellie. *Talking Steel Towns: The Men and Women of America's Steel Valley*. Pittsburgh: Carnegie Mellon University Press, 2007.

Index

African Americans, 33, 40, 44, 58, 72, 82–83, 94, 105, 126, 141, 152; and racism in the mills, 23, 24, 33, 151
Alcohol and alcoholism, 16, 60, 69, 71, 100, 105, 117, 124, 125, 126, 131, 133
Allison, Dorothy, 67, 68
Antigay violence. *See* Gay-bashing
Anxiety, 27, 125–28, 130, 143; about being discovered as gay, 52, 153; as a psychological state, 62, 124
ArcelorMittal, 18, 31, 37, 101

Bars/gay bars, 9, 14, 74, 103, 126, 143, 156
Bérubé, Allan, 65, 69, 149, 151
Blacks. *See* African Americans
Butches/butchness, 12, 26, 55, 67, 77, 79, 91, 92, 93, 98

Cancer, 16, 30, 70, 83, 111, 112, 124, 131
Chauncey, George, 79, 115–16, 120
Chicago, Ill., 13, 28, 29, 36, 41, 143
Childhood sexual abuse, 10, 131, 132, 133, 143
Children of GLBT people. *See* Parents, queer
Coming out, 6, 7, 26, 52, 67, 69, 70, 108, 153, 157; at work, 16, 18, 45, 48, 62, 73, 74, 159

Death and dying. *See* Mortality
D'Emilio, John, 52, 57, 58
District 31 Women's Caucus (USW), 147, 151
Drag performance, 13–14, 74, 107, 119–20, 133
Drugs, illegal, 26, 60, 64, 124

EEOC (Equal Employment Opportunity Commission), 60, 148
Environmental regulations/EPA (Environmental Protection Agency), 3, 32, 34, 37, 111, 112, 131

Family, 2, 40, 59–60, 81, 110, 125, 126, 129, 135, 145, 149; the mill as, 39, 48, 49, 54, 56, 94, 123, 159; and "traditional" values, 6, 23, 105
Feminism/feminists, 67, 109, 118
Firing. *See* Termination of employment

Gary, Ind., 1, 2, 19, 31, 33. *See also* Indiana, Northwest
Gay bars. *See* Bars/gay bars
Gay-bashing, 10, 18, 44, 67, 69, 106, 125, 133, 155; antigay violence as part of mill culture, 30, 48, 50, 58, 65, 124, 153
Gay Pride/Pride parades, 107, 148, 149, 154, 159
Gay rights. *See* Political movements/ gay rights
Grievances and grievance committees. *See* Union stewards

Halberstam, J., 1, 17, 76, 79, 92, 94, 120, 121
HIV and AIDS, 67, 148, 156
Hollibaugh, Amber, 6, 66, 68

Indiana, Northwest, 8, 9, 15, 20, 21, 34, 67, 159
Insecurity. *See* Low self-esteem

Job security, 28, 35, 66, 69

Johnson, E. Patrick, 1, 28, 106

Kennedy, Elizabeth, and Madeline E. Davis, 28, 50, 55, 79, 92

LaTour, Jane, 143, 152
Laws/legal protections for queers, 15, 57, 60, 75, 137, 149, 150
Lay-offs. *See* Termination of employment
Low self-esteem, 35, 70, 102, 131, 153

Management, 25, 30, 34, 35, 43, 73, 80, 123, 135, 144, 146, 152
Media, 15, 69, 102, 115
Mesothelioma, 31, 113, 130
Middle class, 15, 40, 69, 107, 108, 116, 120, 134, 153; attitudes/bias toward, 67, 102, 115, 149, 159
Military, 60, 160
Mortality, 30, 64, 113, 122–36, 159

Newton, Esther, 91, 92, 102–3, 106, 119, 149

Oral history, 8, 12, 28, 29, 41, 109, 139–40, 158

Parents, queer, 23, 25, 28, 40, 136, 141
Political movements/gay rights, 16, 52, 66, 67, 69, 137, 140, 147, 148, 152
Pornography, 12, 80, 90–91, 144
Pride, 2, 10, 61, 68, 76, 109, 153; in mill work, 78, 83, 93, 111, 112, 113, 160
Puerala, Alice, 41–42

Rape, 10, 11, 16, 58, 59, 60, 63, 64, 78, 90, 131, 132
Religion, 32–33, 143
Retirement, 10, 37, 61, 69, 73, 111, 124, 133
Risk-taking, 30, 110

Safety, 4, 24, 40, 60, 93, 96, 112, 123, 127, 159; policies and regulations

regarding, 20, 22, 34, 37, 49, 111, 150
Sedgwick, Eve Kosofsky, 25, 160
Self-confidence. *See* Pride
Sex/sexual behavior, 7, 16, 24, 25, 27, 29, 39, 50–53, 55, 58, 61, 91, 100, 102–6, 110, 115, 119–21; queer sexual pleasures, 30, 87, 94, 116, 153; workplace discussion of, 45, 49, 52, 77, 88
Sexual abuse. *See* Childhood sexual abuse
Sexual harassment, 45, 49, 78, 84, 147
Showers and shower houses, 21, 40, 50–56, 59, 61, 65, 68, 100, 103, 104
Stigmas, 25, 26, 56, 116, 119, 130, 140
Straight people, 25, 41, 50, 52, 72, 73, 80, 81, 82, 88, 89, 92, 97, 99, 104, 106, 116, 119, 134, 149, 151, 152, 155; and gays passing for straight, 48, 53, 65, 79, 142; and presumption of straightness, 85, 102, 113, 130, 143
Stress, 16, 23, 40, 47, 60, 79, 117, 127, 130; caused by hazardous work, 101, 124, 127, 160; over hiding GLBT identity, 4, 48, 58, 69–70, 100, 126, 134, 143. *See also* Anxiety
Swing shift, 23, 47, 134, 136

Termination of employment, 45, 63, 69–70, 100, 118, 156
Trailer parks, 27, 66
Transgender, 8, 54, 58, 117, 156

Union stewards, 42, 66, 142, 144, 150, 151, 152, 155
United States Steel/USX, 18, 19, 22, 31, 41, 54, 58, 60, 75, 152, 154, 160
Urban GLBT populations, 1, 6, 13, 17, 21, 31, 66, 77, 107–8, 120, 149, 156
USW/USWA (United Steelworkers/ United Steelworkers of America), 16, 30, 42, 55, 95, 143, 146, 148, 150, 154, 155; anti-GLBT policies of, 66, 140, 147; history of, 75, 137, 138, 141, 151